TEEN PSYCHIC

Exploring Your Intuitive
Spiritual Powers

Julie Tallard Johnson

Bindu Books
Rochester, Vermont

Bindu Books
One Park Street
Rochester, Vermont 05767
www.InnerTraditions.com

Bindu Books is a division of Inner Traditions International

Library of Congress Cataloging-in-Publication Data

Johnson, Julie Tallard.
  Teen psychic : exploring your intuitive spiritual powers / Julie
Tallard Johnson.
      p. cm.
Summary: Discusses how teenagers can develop their own intuitive powers
and apply those powers to their personal spiritual journeys. Includes
quizzes, exercises, meditations, and other related activities.
Includes bibliographical references and index.
  ISBN 0-89281-094-7
 1. Teenagers—Religious life. 2. Spiritual life. 3. Intuition. [1.
Spiritual life. 2. Intuition.] I. Title.

  BL625.47.J63 2003
  131'.0835—dc22

                                    2003020882

Printed and bound in Canada at Transcontinental

10 9 8 7 6 5 4 3 2 1

Text design and layout by Mary Anne Hurhula
This book was typeset in Veljovic with Papyrus as the display typeface

✇ Contents

A Bird does not sing because it has an answer—it sings because it has a song.

—CHINESE PROVERB

✆ Foreword
Letter from a Teen Psychic

Communication has always been difficult for me. I often felt loud, annoying, and high-strung around adults. I was a gawky, uncoordinated girl with huge glasses, alienated from the bulk of my class. So, just after the start of sixth grade, I retreated into myself.

As a teenager, I felt susceptible to peer pressure and I was overly concerned as to how others saw me. I began to let others run away with my life, losing sight of my own dreams and ideas.

My inability to communicate my internal energy and thoughts frustrated the people around me. A teacher at my high school helped me realize how damaging this was to my relationships and to myself. As a result of this realization I began a search I call "Looking for Myself." My intention was to determine what was true for me, to figure out where I was and what I was going to do. I read many books, painted many pictures, and filled up many notebooks. I meditated. I attended a Senior Rites of Passage discussion group. I spent a great deal of time trying to determine what it was I was looking for, and what I wanted.

Through Julie's book, the one you are about to read, I began the process of communicating with *myself*. Being in touch with myself allows me to realize what I'm feeling and thinking—what I want.

Being conscious of my own thoughts and energy lightens my body and soul; I am less confused and pulled off track by the intentions of others. This consciousness allows me, as it will allow you, to embrace your unique journey and path.

For me, thoughts and feelings are best conveyed through my writing and through living my own life according to the individual truth that is right for me. This book is about helping you find more of that truth for yourself. You may find many helpful tools in this book, as I have—all of which have led me to a stronger sense of self and purpose.

My hope for you is that this book will help you find your own truths. Your truths will nurture your existence and feed your mind, body, and soul. Your truths will enable you to cultivate a fulfilling life.

The journey is never done. I hope we all succeed at moving swiftly and surely toward our dreams as we begin our independent lives. As I am writing this letter, I am preparing to head out West to begin my physical journey of exploration, and then go on to college to learn journalism. I take with me many internal tools from this book. With every step I am a little closer to my true destination—myself.

HAILEY ROESSLER

*This book is dedicated to the memory of my generous father,
Robert Henry Johnson, and to Colleen Brenzy, for passing
on the teachings.*

*Dear reader, you and I may never meet, but I hope my words and
teachings will empower you as the words of so many unmet teachers have empowered me—Pema Chödrön, Chögyam Trungpa, John Sanford, Lama Surya Das,
Black Elk, and Carolyn Myss.
I remain always grateful to the Great Spirit who creates through us all,
to the trees that give of their wood, and to my Spirit Guides who kept me
safe through my teen years.*

ACKNOWLEDGMENTS

I want to first acknowledge all the teens who shared their stories and who gave this book its life—thank you. I also wish to express my thanks to the 2003 Seniors Rites of Passage group in Spring Green, Wisconsin; to a most amazing and inspiring high school teacher, Bob Weinswig; and to Hailey Roessler, whose words and wisdom you will find in this book.

If it weren't for the beautiful and inspiring places where I am fortunate enough to write and "journey," this book would only be an idea. So, thank you to my most wonderful husband for building a home where inspiration is the only possibility. Thanks also to Todd and Karin Miller for having the vision to open up the General Store in Spring Green, where many gather to swap stories (special thanks to David W. Rozelle for your swap). And always to my daughter, Lydia, I owe my heartfelt thanks for her patience and spirit.

I also want to thank the publishing folks who made this book a reality: Ehud Sperling, for putting Bindu Books out into the world; my editor, Vickie Trihy (you are awesome!), for her skill and attention; Jon Graham, who continues to speak up for the creative spirit; Jeanie Levitan, for her formative eye; Mary Anne Hurhula, for her intriguing book design; Peri Champine for the inviting cover; and Jess Matthews and Doris Troy for hunting down and eliminating technical errors. And much appreciation to Donna Dressen, teen mom *extraor-dinaire*, who created much of the art on these pages.

"For long years I have kept this beauty within me.
It has been my life.
It is sacred.
I give it now that coming generations may know
the truth . . ."

—DINÉ, "SANDOVAL'S PRAYER,"
TRANSLATED BY AILEEN O'BRYAN

ᔚ Introduction
Trusting What You Feel

I am going to share with you a secret. A family secret. It's one of those secrets no one has to tell you to keep—you just know not to speak about it. I am beginning with a family secret (you may have one like it) because often where there are secrets, there are treasures to be found. For me, the treasure was my intuition. There's a good chance that much of your intuitive power lies hidden inside you, like a treasure waiting to be discovered.

I knew this secret for a long time, but I didn't fully understand what I knew until my early twenties. When I was seven years old I began to have this sense, this feeling, that someone was missing in our family. Every time we gathered for our occasional family dinner or for a holiday I would be very aware of this missing presence. I would look around me at the dinner table, asking myself, *Who is missing?* and *Where is this feeling coming from?* Years later, when I began to keep a journal, I would write these experiences down. Even though this perception was persistent, I never spoke about it to anyone.

Where in our culture are we taught how to respond to such feelings? Not in most schools, churches, or homes. However, there was a time when people were taught to value, trust, and develop these feelings. There was a time—and I believe it is returning—when young people entering their teens were given special instruction to develop their intuitive and spiritual powers. They were taught to understand their bodies not only as muscle, blood, and bone, but also as energy and containers of the spirit. They learned how to use their own intuitive experiences to reveal the truth about themselves and their world. Understanding these mystical truths was an essential part of the journey to adulthood in ancient cultures.

This ability to access inner wisdom is still valued and practiced in some areas of the world. As Arnold Mindell, author of *The Shaman's Body*, explains, intuitive wisdom relies on being deeply attuned to the body.

"Indigenous healers have taught that the quality of life depends upon body sensations that are linked to dreams and the environment, to what I call the 'shaman's body.' According to medicine people living in native settings around the world, and to mystical traditions, the shaman's dreaming body, when accessed, is a source of health, personal growth, good relationships, and a sense of community."

What Mindell refers to as the shaman's body I will call the energy body. To understand the language of the energy body—your intuition—is to find great strength, wisdom, and freedom. With this book you will learn to speak that language.

When I was a teenager, I had no such understanding—but my energy body was constantly sending me signals just the same. I began to notice that I was often aware of things that were hidden under the surface of my everyday interactions with other people. I had a strong sense of what others were feeling; I felt as though I was seeing into other people's secret worlds and glimpsing their hidden treasures. I

seemed to know a lot more about what was going on around me than people were telling me. I often had psychic dreams—dreams that gave me more insight into what was happening in my life. And perhaps the most perplexing signal, the sensation that someone was missing from our family, only increased as the years went by.

At age twenty-five, I had an opportunity to test the validity of this particular feeling. My father was visiting me, and it felt like the right time to share my secret. I began by telling my father what I understood at the time about intuition (I had by that time investigated this topic in a variety of ways). I told him of the many intuitive markers in my life, when my feeling sense—my wisdom body—had alerted me to the truth about something. And finally I described my intuitive experiences during family time.

He listened and I could sense his heart open to me. He sat very still with his full attention on me as I spoke. Then I asked him the question that had troubled me since childhood: Did he have any other children? His answer was open and kind. I could see that in this moment he, too, needed to speak his truth. He told me that, yes, he had another daughter. She was born when I was seven years old.

I felt such love as the truth in my heart was finally validated by my father. He gave me the greatest gifts a father can give—his truths and his recognition. A weight I carried in my heart and body lifted, and a great peace entered and filled me. We sat and ate together, but nothing at that meal tasted as sweet and wonderful as my father's honesty.

So much came together for me then. This validation of my intuition opened a door within me that has remained wide open ever since. The truth really does set one free. Now I was free to fully trust my intuitive self. I knew that there would always be truth to be discovered if I had the wisdom and courage to listen for it. Now I was

"Clear intuition requires the ability to respect your own impressions."
—CAROLINE MYSS, MEDICAL INTUITIVE, AUTHOR OF *ANATOMY OF THE SPIRIT*

"Children are wise, even if adults cannot see it. We are so obsessed with teaching them that we do not notice what masters they really are."
—VICTOR SANCHEZ, AUTHOR OF *THE TOLTEC PATH OF RECAPITULATION*

free to decide what it meant to me to have a half sister. Later in my life, I would go in search of her.

The gift of intuition didn't come without its problems. Being intuitive often meant experiencing an overload of psychic energy from my surroundings, which sometimes made life more painful and difficult. Nothing in my formal education or spiritual practice taught me how to *use and control* my intuition. As a teenager, it helped me a great deal to begin a meditation practice and to consult the I Ching. I also found it useful to write down my dreams and reflect on their meaning. I kept a journal of my psychic as well as my more mundane life experiences.

Yet, this was not enough. These practices did not speak directly enough to my intuitive feelings and experiences. They didn't advise me about how to use my own energy body, or how to respond to the energy of other people, or how to recognize intuitive wisdom. Books on intuitive development, such as Caroline Myss's *Anatomy of the Spirit,* didn't come out for another fifteen years.

I was already in my mid-thirties when my spiritual adviser and psychologist told me about a local psychic and healer who taught a yearlong psychic development class. At the age of thirty-five, I attended this class and finally got the instruction I needed. A void in my life was being filled. I came to understand so much about myself, my feelings, and my intuitive body—my wisdom body. I felt so strongly that the material in the class should be shared with more people that I began to teach the class myself, and to this day I continue to teach it. Now, with this book, I can share with you the ideas and techniques for intuitive development that I have learned over the past fifteen years.

These are subjects of great importance not typically taught to young people. Many of the teenagers I come in contact with are troubled by social anxiety and feeling overly sensitive. Some speak about

ⴻⵌ ⴻⵌ ⴻⵌ

"I disappoint some people when I discuss intuition because I firmly believe that intuitive or symbolic sight is not a gift but a skill—a skill based in self-esteem."

—CAROLINE MYSS,
AUTHOR OF
ANATOMY OF THE SPIRIT

ⴻⵌ ⴻⵌ ⴻⵌ

feeling some kind of "instinct," but they doubt themselves too much to act on it. Many talk about getting "signs" but are not sure how to interpret them. All of these concerns can be alleviated dramatically by understanding and developing your intuition.

There are now many quality books on intuitive development for adults, but none especially for teenagers. This book provides you with tools for developing the intuitive powers you will need as you make your way through the powerful passage to adulthood. It is a guide that will take you on a journey: into your own wisdom body and onto the path of the visionary. This time in your life, when you are discovering all of your powers and unique qualities, is an ideal time to begin to walk this path. It is also a time to begin to move through the fears and obstacles keeping you from discovering these treasures. It is time to tap into the powerful source of wisdom and guidance that was given to you at birth.

Every One of Us Has Intuition

To some degree, you and every other person on earth has this spiritual perception, this skill. For me it was very intense; for others it is quite subtle. It doesn't matter if it is strong or faint—what matters is that you learn how to listen to it. As you read this book, you will find many exercises and ideas on how to recognize and develop your intuition further.

Some Basics about Intuition

It doesn't benefit anyone for you to be less than you are. To not use your intuition is to be less than you are. To not know and live by your own truths is being less than you are. To ignore your energy body is being less than you are. To be *everything* that you are, and were meant to be, you need to begin by understanding some basic truths about everyone's intuitive powers.

"The intuitive wisdom mind is that of a deeper level of being."
—Stephen Levine, meditation teacher and author of *A Gradual Awakening*

"All of us have intuitive feelings all the time."
—Shakti Gawain, author of *Developing Intuition*

Truth One: Intuition is an ability that we are all given at birth.

Truth Two: You have a right to develop and use your intuitive/psychic ability, particularly at this pivotal time in your life.

Truth Three: Your intuition is your direct connection to spirit (God, Higher Power, the Creator, Goddess, Buddha, the Tao, etc.).

Truth Four: Your intuition is part of the creative energy that flows through us all and through everything.

Truth Five: Your intuition increases as your understanding and love for yourself and others increases.

Truth Six: Emotional intensity is part of your intuitive nature.

Truth Seven: Your intuitive/psychic journey is meant to make you feel powerful and good about yourself.

Truth Eight: When you use your intuition, it benefits everyone.

Truth Nine: Some people are more easily able to use their intuition, just as some are more able with music, but *everyone* can develop his or her intuition.

Truth Ten: Intuitive wisdom and intuitive/psychic development are not "New Age"; they are very "Old Age," respected and taught in ancient cultures in many forms.

In our culture, it can be difficult to access and trust our intuition. Shakti Gawain, author of *Developing Your Intuition*, offers this explanation: "One of the reasons that many of us do not learn to trust and follow our intuition is that we are taught from an early age to try to accommodate those around us, to follow certain rules of behavior, to suppress our spontaneous impulses, and to do what is expected of us." Sound true to you? In school we are constantly reminded to accommodate teachers and authority, to follow the rules, and to suppress our intense emotions—in essence, to do exactly what is expected of us. While these guidelines have an obvious purpose and are in some measure necessary for us all when we are in school, the fact is that they *do* hinder our intuitive abilities. When we habitually look outside ourselves for direction, we don't get to exercise an important life skill: that of listening for—and acting on—our own inner wisdom.

We all need the help and guidance of others. But never should you follow the advice of others when it means to ignore your own inner guidance. There are times when teachers are wrong. Sometimes a friend's advice is misguided. Clergymen and others in positions of trust or authority can abuse their power. We need to listen to our inner guidance while we consider the advice and direction of others. When our inner voice says "No" or "Think about it first," we must listen to it, and find out what it is trying to tell us. As you develop the intuition that is inside of you and learn to think more for yourself, you can go out into the world more aware, confident, and strong.

How to Use This Book

First of all, I invite you to have fun with this book. Let it be an adventure you go on with yourself and, if you choose, with your friends. The exercises and readings I have chosen will guide you on a journey of spiritual discovery that will empower you with truth and courage.

Most of the chapters begin with two stories that illustrate the ideas discussed in the chapter. The first one will be written by or about a teenager, portraying his or her intuitive and spiritual awakening. The second story will be a traditional tale from one of many cultures around the world. These indigenous cultures valued intuition and the spiritual life and believed it was important that elders, such as myself, teach this wisdom to our youth.

"**Don't read with the mind only. Watch out for any 'feeling response' as you read and a sense of recognition from deep within. I cannot tell you any spiritual truth that deep within you don't know already. All I can do is remind you of what you have forgotten. Living knowledge, ancient and yet ever new, is then activated and released from within every cell of your body.**"

—ECKHART TOLLE, FROM *THE POWER OF NOW: A GUIDE TO SPIRITUAL ENLIGHTENMENT*

A Quiz: How Intuitive Are You?

This quiz uses a scoring system to give you a general idea of where you fall right now within a range of intuitive awareness.

There are twenty-three statements below for you to read and respond to. On a separate sheet of paper, write the numbers 1 through 23 in a vertical column. Read each statement. Then, next to the number on your paper that corresponds to that statement, write the word that best describes how often you experience what the statement says. Choose one of these words for your answer: *often, sometimes,* or *rarely.*

1. I am aware of others' feelings.
2. I experience social anxiety.
3. I sense things before they happen.
4. I remember my dreams.
5. I have recurring dreams.
6. I am afraid of some of my feelings.
7. I experience a lot of coincidences.
8. I have gut feelings about decisions.
9. Friends seem to come to me a lot for advice.
10. I know my dreams mean something.
11. I have been told that I am too sensitive, that I overreact.
12. I have déjà vu experiences.
13. I believe I am intuitive.
14. I believe or sense that a greater power watches over me and helps me.
15. I am scared of what I know.
16. I have sensed things were going to happen before they did.
17. I have high self-esteem.
18. I can speak up for myself to my peers.
19. I can speak up for myself to adults.
20. I know how to ask for advice.
21. I have a strong sense of purpose; I know what I am going to do with my life.
22. I use drugs and/or food to avoid my thoughts and feelings.
23. I know when someone is not telling the truth.

Now use the following list to assign points to each of your answers. Determine your score by adding up all the points. Give yourself:

1 point for each time you wrote "rarely"

2 points for each time you wrote "sometimes"

3 points for each time you wrote "often"

If you scored 23 to 35:

You aren't often aware of or tuned in to your intuition. You may sense some inner voice inside of you but you're not sure how to access it. Possibly you don't feel very good about yourself or trust the way you do feel, but this will improve quickly as you practice the exercises in this book. The first step for you will be to start uncovering your hidden intuition and making it more available to you. Soon you will begin noticing a stronger awareness of yourself and your surroundings. You will find that you trust your intuitive self more often and feel more energized and positive. Keeping a journal while you read this book will be very helpful.

If you scored 36 to 58:

You are often in touch with your intuitive sense, although you may not fully understand what it all means. Some people may experience you as oversensitive but friends are likely to come to you for advice because you often have good insight into their problems. You may experience some social anxiety due to your very real sensitivity to the energy around you. You may not always trust or understand your abilities. You may oscillate between times when you have very good feelings about yourself (high self-esteem) and times when you bottom out and your self-esteem is very low.

You will quickly benefit from this book because you will find the guidance contained here makes you feel safer, more balanced, and more confident in your intuitive abilities.

If you scored 59 to 69:

You are very aware that you have psychic abilities although you have not received instruction on how to skillfully use them. Your self-esteem is fairly high most of the time and you are ready for and excited about using the guidance in this book. Your confidence and skills will build quickly as you work through the activities in the ensuing chapters.

Regardless of your score, this book will help you develop and trust what is already inside of you.

The stories will be followed by simple explanations and exercises for understanding and developing your own intuition and energy body. Many of the exercises I learned from others; many I developed myself over the years. Some are techniques that were taught to ancient peoples as they entered their teen years. Practicing these exercises will not only increase your intuitive powers but will increase your creative energy as well. You will notice positive changes in yourself as you progress through the book. You cannot do the suggested activities in this book without a significant increase in your self-esteem, because your intuitive self is the true source of self-esteem.

I recommend that you progress through each chapter in sequence since most of the material in one chapter builds on the previous chapters. However, if you wish, you can just read bits and pieces and try certain exercises that speak to you. Whichever approach you take, you will find that the more you use the wisdom in this book, the more spiritually and intuitively empowered you will become.

Before we go any further, I would like to be clear about what I mean when I use the word *psychic*. *Psychic* comes from the Greek word *psyche,* which is translated as "the soul." It is defined as "sensitive to nonphysical or supernatural forces." So, to be psychic means to be able to hear the language of the soul, to understand the language of energy. It is not about fortune-telling, although having a sense of what the future holds may be a skill of a gifted psychic. Our psychic abilities enable us to tap into the wisdom and power of our souls and energy bodies, and to open up to the spiritual world.

What Is Shamanism?

Throughout this book you will find references to shamanism and shamans. Shamans are spiritual specialists, knowledgeable in matters of spirit and energy. Traditionally, shamans were people believed to have been chosen by spirits, who could enter a trance state and travel into the spirit world. Shamans played a vital role in their communities, dedicating their lives to the betterment of their people. They were sought out for advice, fortune-telling, and healing the sick. Shamans had to undergo a great deal of training and practice with an established shaman before being initiated into service. Thousands of ethnic groups around the world still recognize shamans.

In your own local area, you are likely to find people referring to themselves as "shamanic practitioners" but not necessarily as shamans. Shamanic practitioners use practices such as those found in this book to empower themselves and others spiritually and to make direct contact with the spirit world.

You don't have to be a shaman to practice shamanism. In fact, you will be engaging in shamanic practices throughout this book. You will be opening up to your vital energy and the spirit world that is inside of you and outside of you. Some of you may well become shamans, after you use this book to open the door to the truth about you.

"Basically . . . the shaman uses altered states of consciousness to communicate with and influence the forces of nature and the universe for the benefit of society. In order to do this, the shaman everywhere practices the accumulation of inner power. These are the three most distinguishing features of the shaman, then: the use of altered states; influencing events for social benefit; and the accumulation of inner power."

—SERGE KING, *THE WAY OF THE ADVENTURER*

"The shaman relies on inner powers to support his or her conclusions about a situation, rather than on material concerns which is often the case today,"

—JOSÉ STEVENS AND LENA S. STEVENS, FROM *SECRETS OF SHAMANISM*

"Shamanism itself is a time-honored cross-cultural quest for knowledge and personal power that predates all known religions, psychologies and philosophies."

—JOSÉ STEVENS AND LENA S. STEVENS, *SECRETS OF SHAMANISM*

Keeping Your Psychic Journal

Because there will be changes within you and outside of you, you may want to keep a special psychic journal. Use your journal to document and reflect on your psychic experiences, your dreams, and your intuitive insights. Many of the exercises in this book include answering questions in your journal as well. Some of the personal experiences I share with you in this book are from the many journals I have kept since the age of fifteen.

Forming a Teen Psychic Group/Circle

I recommend that you discuss this book with a friend, mentor, spiritual adviser, therapist, or study group. This will give you someone to share your experiences with as well as someone to listen to any concerns you might have. You may want to form a Teen Psychic group to read the book and do the exercises together. You will find a list of recommended organizations and groups to contact for further guidance and support in the Resources section of this book.

My intention for this book is to help you discover and walk the path that leads to your own truths and gifts—not mine or anybody else's. Along the way you will learn the secrets young people used to know about the energy body, about the wisdom of our intuition and emotions, and about our spirituality. Take from this book whatever you may find helpful. Start walking now. All that you need will arrive to help you.

If you want the truth,
I'll tell you the truth:
Listen to the secret sound,
which is inside you.
—RUMI, SUFI POET

Opening the Door: A Beginning Meditation

Use this exercise to open the door to communication with your body and its energy. It is adapted from a variety of yoga practices, which assist you in awakening the vital energy that is in you.

Lie comfortably on your back on the floor, on a yoga mat or rug, with pillows under your neck and knees. Place your hands loosely at your sides or on top of your belly. For a few moments simply lie still, breathing and relaxing while at the same time staying in tune with your body. Instead of daydreaming, notice the sensations of your body . . . the rhythm of your breathing, the touch of clothes against your skin, the images that appear in your mind's eye . . . relax, breathe, and remain present, just lying on the floor, relaxed yet present. Notice the different parts of your body and, without judgment, bring your awareness to them. Begin with your legs, relaxing them even more, letting them rest from their constant exertion. Now bring your awareness to your waist and lower torso, perhaps noticing the breath and how it makes the belly rise and fall . . . Notice the arms relaxed at your sides; allow them to sink into the floor. Relax even more . . . yet maintain a presence in the body. Bring your awareness to your entire torso and then up to your chest. Notice your spine and relax it into the floor . . . continue to breathe and relax. Notice your shoulders and neck, inviting them too to relax as you bring your awareness to them . . . Allow your head to rest heavily on the pillow, breathing and relaxing in awareness of your body . . .

After a few minutes of this relaxed presence in your body, take a moment to notice what it feels like to be alert and relaxed at the same time . . . without judgment (no right and wrong), just notice. Rest as long as you like in this state of awareness. Then take a couple of deep breaths and sit up. You may want to take a moment to write what you experienced in your journal.

"If you're an alive body, no one can tell you how to experience the world. And no one can tell you what truth is, because you experience it for yourself. The body does not lie."
—STANLEY KELEMAN, AUTHOR OF *LOVE: A SOMATIC VIEW*

"Peoples of ancient times and indigenous peoples of the present have chosen different ways, and that is why we have so much to learn from them. They have not separated themselves from the silent knowledge, the knowledge of the energetic body, as we have done."
—VICTOR SANCHEZ, TOLTEC MEDICINE MAN

I listened to the singer's song
he sang of old times
and I found the path.

—Maurice Kenny, poet,
taken from *Akwesan Notes*

1
A Desire for Light
Claiming Your Intuitive Powers

◉ AUGUST'S STORY ◉

My parents gave me this name, August, because I was born in that month. I've come to like my name. My parents are loving, kind, hard-working parents, and all through my teen years (I'm twenty-one now) we got along. While most of my friends were fighting with their parents, I was enjoying my parents' company.

My mother is an award-winning artist and she has dreams for me to be an artist as well. In my sophomore year of high school, she set up an art studio in the small northeastern town we live in. That year, I began to teach art to young children. In my senior year my mother told me that she was going to give me the studio. By then I was very busy teaching classes after school and working hard at finishing up high school myself, and I wasn't sure how I would be able to help run the studio with so much going on. What I was doing was very exciting to me, and I also knew how much it meant to my mother to be able to give me the studio. It was at this time that I began getting these funny sensations in my gut, and at times would have anxiety attacks. By the end of my senior year I was diagnosed with uterine ulcers.

The first four years of the art school were a success, although very stressful for both my mother and me. After graduating I had to get another job because the costs of running the school were very high. I began to work at a local preschool, teaching art and crafts. I was also taking a college course over the Internet. Even though I appeared happy and successful, I continued to have anxiety and my ulcers were getting much worse.

I kept having the feeling that something wasn't right. But what could possibly be wrong? It had to be me. I thought, something is wrong with me. Soon my parents helped me buy a house with a cousin of mine, and by the age of eighteen I was running a business, working two jobs, taking an Internet class, and making payments on a house and a car. I still didn't feel happy. I had been thrown into my adult life and I just didn't feel ready for all that was happening. I was getting sicker and sicker.

I went to several doctors and all they could do was tell me to cut down on stress and give me medication for my ulcers and anxiety. It was even suggested that I have my uterus removed. Finally, one of my mother's friends suggested I go to an intuitive healer. I thought it sounded a little strange but it felt right and I was real curious. I really wanted to feel better.

I was nineteen when I went to Julie. First she sat with me for a while and let me know she was going to listen to her wisdom body and connect with mine. She looked as if she was meditating and then began to speak to me: "Your body has a wisdom of its own and is trying to tell you something. Something in your life is giving you a bellyache. Something in your life is giving you these ulcers and anxiety. Listen to these symptoms—they are messengers."

She asked me if I knew what the message was that my body was trying to send me. I wasn't sure. I knew she was right—that something was trying to get my attention. It was more than stress. Then Julie asked if she could do some healing work with me. She explained that this meant she would be placing her hands gently on my belly and asking me some ques-

tions. I agreed. While I was lying down she placed her hands gently on my belly. As she touched me I could feel the heat of her hands through my clothes. Then she asked me to listen to my belly—she kept telling me to "breathe and listen; breathe and listen."

It seemed that everything but her hands and my breath and belly disappeared. She had me breathing and listening for at least fifteen minutes, when something in me just seemed to break open. It's as if I could feel a great door opening inside of me and I began to cry. I'm not sure how long I cried, but when I was done, I felt exhausted and relieved. Her hands were still on my belly, and when I looked up I could see she was smiling right into my soul. And then she asked me, "What did your belly tell you?" And even though it was very scary to say this out loud, it was the truth— I told Julie that my belly told me to stop living my mother's dream and go live my own.

I met with Julie several times as I gradually gave up my mother's dream and started living my own. The most difficult part was feeling like I was disappointing my mother. I so wanted to please her. That was part of my bellyache and anxiety too—I always want to please others, at the expense of my own well-being. And, Julie explained, intuitively I knew what others wanted. Fortunately, my mother got through her disappointment and supported my decision to go away to art college. I knew if I waited too long, I would never go. Perhaps I will come back some day and run a school—but that is a long way off.

I no longer have ulcers and the anxiety is almost entirely gone. It comes up when I feel I have to make sure that I am making others happy. I am still working on not being a full-time pleaser! And I am practicing not automatically doing what I intuitively know others want from me. (Julie explains that even though we know what others want, this doesn't mean they can have it!) I take the time to consider what I want and check things out with others before assuming what they expect of me. I am now attending art *college in another state. I work a few hours a week teaching art to kids but most of my time goes to schoolwork. I use the material in this book to build my intuitive and creative skills and I know it has helped my art.*

I recently painted a self-portrait for a class. It is an image of me, walking through a large doorway toward a mirror.

⊚ Desire for Light ⊚
A Mackenzie Delta Eskimo story
from *Northern Tales*, selected by Howard Norman

There was once a small boy whose father was dead and only his mother was left to look after him. The other people in the place constantly ill-treated him and made his childhood miserable. Years rolled by, and he grew older and stronger. One winter the people in the village built a large dance-house where they used to gather every evening. The boy spent nearly all his time in the open air; even while the others stayed in the dance house, he would often be wandering about outside.

One evening when he was gazing around outside as usual, he saw a bright light, so he started out and walked for a very long time till at last he reached a big dance-house. He was gazing in through the window, but someone inside called out, "What are you standing out there for? Come inside." So inside he went. Men were sitting all around on three sides of the room, and the boy took his place on the fourth side near the door. Time after time the men asked him whether he were not a shaman, and each time he would answer, "No I am not a shaman."

Finally, a man sitting opposite him on the platform said, "No, you are not a shaman; you are only a poor orphan boy, whom everyone ill-treats. I know all about you and I should like to help you." Then, getting down from the platform, he turned to another man and said, "Bring me my seal spear and my ice-scratcher." The man went out and brought them in. The shaman said, "My spirit, help me. Make ice appear in the floor." A moment later a tiny circle of ice appeared in the middle of the floor, and gradually widened until it covered the whole space. A seal-hole opened up in the middle, and a seal emerged and crawled out onto the edge of the ice. The shaman crept up and speared it, cut it up, and distributed it among all the people in the dance-house except the boy. Then the ice disappeared and the floor came back.

The shaman asked the boy if he wished to see more, but the boy was too frightened to answer. "You are a poor boy," the shaman continued, "and I should like to help you. Soon it will be light and then it will be too late. Shall I do some more?" In a voice barely audible the boy managed to whisper, "Yes." The shaman immediately called out, "My spirit, help me." The floor became covered with young ice pierced with a row of holes through which a fishing net was set. The shaman drew it in—it was full of whitefish, which he laid out on the ice to freeze, then divided up among the people on the platform as before. Once again the ice vanished and the house resumed its usual appearance. Again the shaman called out, "My spirit, help me." This time a moor appeared, and a ring of nooses into which caribou were driven and caught; these too the shaman divided up among the people.

Before daylight the boy was sent home. A short time afterwards when all the people of his village were gathered in the dance-house one evening, someone said to him, "You play us something, too." Then the boy thought to himself, "Why did everyone over there ask me if I were a shaman? I am not a shaman, but if they are going to call me a shaman, I may as well act like one." So he sat down in the middle of the floor and called, "My spirit, help me." Everyone remained silent, watching to see what would happen. Presently the floor turned into ice and a seal appeared, which he speared, cut up, and distributed among the people for them to eat. Afterwards, all the people of his village were afraid of him. He was a great shaman.

CALLING TO SPIRIT FOR HELP: CLAIMING YOUR BIRTHRIGHT

Both the above stories are about young adults claiming their intuitive powers—their birthright. Like the young people in the stories, you too have a right to follow and express your intuition. The practice of claiming our intuition is really about tapping into our inner wisdom—claiming our life fully, *all* of who we are. To whatever degree you are intuitive, claiming it fully will only enhance your life. Once we can listen to the truth of our wisdom-bodies, our intuition, life becomes a wonderful adventure of the soul. This chapter will help you begin to claim what has always been yours to claim.

"Everything that is alive pulsates with energy and all of this energy contains information."

—CAROLINE MYSS, MEDICAL INTUITIVE, AUTHOR OF *ANATOMY OF THE SPIRIT*

"We Sioux believe that there is something within us that controls us, something like a second person almost. We call it *nagi*, what other people might call soul, spirit, or essence. One can't see it, touch it or taste it."

—LAME DEER, FROM *LAME DEER: SEEKER OF VISIONS*

To use our powers we must first become *aware of* and open to them. My life changed when I learned how to listen to my intuitive self— the nagi, the spirit inside me. Once I started listening to that spirit and trusting it, my life opened up. And yours will too. When August began to listen to her wisdom-body, she started living her own dream. When the Eskimo boy dared to claim his powers as a shaman, he was able to feed his village and gain respect. Many stories in this book will introduce you to young people who discovered what was possible for them when they listened to that inner voice.

The stories also warn us that *not* living by our inner knowing will bring unnecessary suffering and confusion. What do you think would have happened to August had she *not* listened to her body's wisdom? What do you think the future would have looked like for the boy if he had not brought out what was inside of him? Lies exhaust us. Have you noticed how it takes more energy to live a lie than it does to live our truth? Have you ever kept a secret and noticed how much you wanted to express it to someone? *To keep a secret takes energy.* To keep your intuition down takes energy too. To fight who you truly are—to *not* live your own dream—means to have your body ache for you to live your own life. Are you living a parent's dream for you, rather than your own?

It may be difficult, even painful for a while, to live your truth. August was worried and sad for her mother; I began to miss my sister whom I never knew. But living our truth doesn't drain our energy, or cause ulcers. This journey you are beginning is really about *bringing forth what you already have inside of you.* This is what Jesus surely meant when he spoke these words from the Gospel according to Thomas: "If you bring forth what is inside of you, what is inside of you will save you; if you do not bring forth what is inside of you, what is inside of you will destroy you."

Your inner wisdom can show you things in yourself that you would never have guessed were there. In this book I will teach you what my spiritual teachers taught me—to claim and use your inner wisdom so your life becomes aligned with who you are.

THE ENERGY BODY: LISTENING TO YOUR *NAGI*

The healers of ancient cultures taught their people that everything has a vital energy, including our bodies. In Hindu culture this energy

"We can view our bodies as manifestations of spiritual energy."

—CHRISTIANE NORTHRUP, M.D., AUTHOR OF *WOMEN'S BODIES, WOMEN'S WISDOM*

"Ever since I was a little boy, I dreamed I would do something important in aviation."

—NEIL ARMSTRONG, AMERICAN ASTRONAUT

is called *prana;* in Chinese it is referred to as *qi* and in Japanese *ki.* The Kabbalists (Jewish mystics) speak of it as "astral light," while in Tibetan culture this vital energy is called *vayu.* Australian Aborigines refer to our "dreaming bodies," and as mentioned earlier in this chapter the Sioux call it *nagi.* In our own culture we commonly refer to this energy as our "essence" or our "energy body." All these terms are referring to the same entity: our intuition—the invisible, nonphysical energy we all have inside of us, our inner wisdom. You may have experienced it as a sensitivity, a gut feeling, a hunch, a knowing, an instinct, a vibration, a perception, an altered state, a premonition, an awareness. These are all ways that this energy speaks to us. That gut feeling comes from the nagi within you—the spirit that is you.

Every living thing is made of energy. This means that everything can be understood *energetically* (intuitively). Even our thoughts have energy. You have probably heard that what is first created in thought is later manifested in life. That is the basis for the common expression "Be careful what you wish for, you just might get it." (Read more about this in chapter 6: Anything Is Possible.) When you can understand and connect with this energy and trust your intuition, it will lead you to where you need to go—whether that means finding a half sister, going off to college, or discovering that you, too, are a shaman.

The Language of Energy

Learning the language of energy is learning the language of the soul. As we learn to "read" energy, we come to experience the truth about ourselves and the world around us, because *energy always speaks the truth.*

Our inner wisdom is always, always trying to reach us. When we don't listen to it, it goes "underground"—into our bodies and our subconscious mind. It hides in our dreams and in our thoughts. When it goes underground, it can cause us emotional pain or even physical ill-

"Don't be satisfied with these stories, how things have gone for others. Unfold your own myth, without complicated explanation, so everyone will understand the passage, *'We have opened you.'"*

—RUMI, SUFI POET

"It takes more energy to walk in a lie than in our truth."

—COLLEEN BRENZY, INTUITIVE HEALER, PHILOSOPHER

ness. In August's case her intuition went underground into her uterus, and that was how it finally got her attention. We could say that her uterus carried her truth. In my story, my subconscious mind carried my knowing—it constantly nudged me until I spoke up. I also had dreams that spoke my truth to me. And I had underground truths in my body as well. Until the age of twenty-seven I suffered from a spastic colon. Once I began trusting and practicing my intuitive skills and living my truth, the spasms went away and never returned.

Any of the following symptoms can be messages that our truth is going underground:

- headache
- fatigue
- anxiety
- depression
- eating disorder
- ulcers
- chronic pain
- addiction
- body aches and pains

A lack of connection with your intuition may not be the only cause of such ailments, and it may be wise to discuss them with a medical professional. However, I can promise you that connecting with your intuition and your wisdom-body will help heal them.

If you have recurring problems with any of the above conditions, you may want to begin right now, in this moment, to communicate with your body. When we are in pain we typically tighten around the sore spot and hold our breath, resulting in more stress and pain in that area and throughout

"Regardless of where the initiation into human mysteries takes place, it always feels like more than you can handle. Even though you are right here with everyone and everything else, it is as if you were walking upon another planet, and you are afraid even to trust your own body."
—ARNOLD MINDELL, PSYCHOLOGIST, AUTHOR OF *THE SHAMAN'S BODY*

"In times of universal deceit, telling the truth is truly a revolutionary act."
—GEORGE ORWELL, ENGLISH NOVELIST AND SOCIAL CRITIC

the body. You can soften the area around it by "breathing" into it. When we imagine breathing into that area, it loosens up the tension and gives the wound space to heal.

Touch the part of your body that hurts and tell it, "I am listening." Breathe into that part of you that hurts. Tell this hurting part of you that you will be taking better care of it. And breathe . . . breathe into the part that hurts, and let it know that you are here, listening.

The Truth Will Set You Free

Your body and your soul are always trying to find a way to express the truth. In fact, the soul uses the body to communicate with you. Can you imagine how sick a dog would get if it tried to be a cat? That may sound like an extreme example, but it's no different from a person trying to live a life that is not based on his or her true nature. Each of us contains our truths—contains all the possibility of who we are and what we can become. The truth in you will fight for expression. So you need to learn to read the language of the soul. You need to become skillful at listening to your own energy and to your own body's language.

My mother wanted me to be a dancer. So I took a few dance classes in college. And I do love to dance. But I was born to do other things. I was born to heal, and to teach and to write. When I started honoring all these truths about me, I became free. Free to heal. Free to teach. Free to write. August is now free to paint and to teach. Who knows what else will open up for her as she continues to listen to the language of her energy body?

How is your body feeling as you read these words? What truth is your body trying to tell you?

"Altered states of consciousness are a very natural and normal part of everyday life. When entered with intention, they allow access to information not usually available in normal states of consciousness."
—ALAN SEALE, INTERFAITH MINISTER, AUTHOR OF *INTUITIVE LIVING*

"Truth is tough. It will not break, like a bubble, at a touch. Nay, you may kick it about all day, and it will be round and full at evening."
—OLIVER WENDELL HOLMES, PHYSICIAN, POET, AND HUMORIST

Getting in Touch with Your Energy Body

Make a Friendship Pact With Your Body

Talk to your body. Consider what it needs and wants. Be kind and caring toward this container of your soul. Keep it safe. Treat your body as you would a best friend. Ground yourself every day (see page 37). This simple technique will bring your awareness into your body.

Journal Your Impressions and Responses

Respond in your journal to the suggestions and questions in this book. Jasmine's journal entries about listening to her energy body brought an important issue into focus for her.

> *"It was through my journaling that I began to get a true grip on what was really wrong. I noticed that I would have headaches only on the days I returned to my family's farm. I was scared at first to write down my dreams that I had of killing my parents but realized just how angry I was at them and how I had to do something to heal from this. Ignoring it was only making me feel worse. Once I started to listen to my anger and work on this, my relationships got better and the headaches came less often."*
>
> —Jasmine, age 19

Consider keeping two notebooks. I suggest having one large one at home, where you can draw and write responses to the questions in this book. Use this home journal to explore the feelings, beliefs, and experiences that arise as you interact with this new material. You may also want to journal any past dreams or experiences you consider intuitive.

"Of all the disciplines of magic, the art of moving energy is the simplest and most natural. It comes as easily as breathing, as making sound. Picture the power in motion, and it moves. Feel it flowing, and it flows, cleansing, healing, renewing, and revitalizing as it passes."

—STARHAWK, RITUAL GUIDE, AUTHOR OF *THE SPIRAL DANCE*

The second journal would be a pocket journal to begin recording your intuitive experiences during the day. Take this journal everywhere with you.

Possible entries for your pocket journal:

- Coincidences and synchronicities
- Feelings that seem to be connected to the wisdom-body (anxiety, for example)
- Gut feelings
- Intuitive sensations (a feeling about something)
- Hunches
- Experiences of déjà vu (a sense that you have had this exact same experience before)
- Times when you feel sensitive
- Questions that keep coming up in your mind
- Times when you know what others are feeling
- Recurring thoughts (i.e., "This person really likes me." "Beware of that person.")
- *Any* thoughts, feelings, and experiences that you think may be intuitive

Remember to let this be *fun*. Write anything and everything you feel relates to your intuition. Simply bringing this awareness to your intuition will develop it.

Relate to Yourself as an Energy Body

Begin to notice and pay attention to *energy*. How does it feel to be with a certain person? Notice when you have intuitive feelings such as hunches, gut feelings, a repetitive thought. Notice your

"Experience is not what happens to you; it is what you do with what happens to you."

—ALDOUS HUXLEY, AUTHOR, PHILOSOPHER

"The insights that arise in the wisdom mind are often experienced as sudden, wordless understandings of how things are."

—STEPHEN LEVINE, MEDITATION TEACHER, AUTHOR OF *A GRADUAL AWAKENING*

nergy would you say these

tions, without judging them
ndation to intuitive develop- now your body feels, you will
l learn more about the energy

be open to your intuition and open to your energy ... your soul the message that you value your intuitive and spiritual self.

What is this precious love and laughter
Budding in our hearts?
It is the glorious sound
Of a soul waking up!

—HAFIZ, SUFI MASTER,
FROM *THE GIFT*

"Una Ko la ti   e la wo quu
I go gwo du u hi   do ti gwa la sgu
Gu wa du hnu hu hi   i gu gwo du u hi

I am beautiful!
Like the yellow Rainbow,
From my feet up,
I am beautiful."

—CHEROKEE SONG FROM
THE PATH TO SNOWBIRD MOUNTAIN

2
Awakening Your Rainbow Body

◎ Tammi's Story ◎

I was raised in a family where my dad worked long hours and drank a lot. He didn't really have all that much time for us. My mother ran the house, got us off to school, took us to our many events, and kept my dad and us fed. I was alone a lot, and my brother abused me by doing everything he could to scare me.

I was around thirteen or fourteen when I had this experience of "coming into my body." A lot of people mention "out-of-body experiences" but this experience was me noticing my self coming into my body. I was sitting in the backseat of the car as my parents were driving us all somewhere. It happened in an instant—I felt myself come in and noticed that up until then I must have been off somewhere else. What struck me is that I must have spent a lot of time not in my body. And even though I remember this being a positive experience, in many ways my life got more difficult for a while. I became overly sensitive to the energy around me. I was always aware of what others were thinking and feeling. I felt like a layer of skin had been taken off and I could feel everything more intensely.

As I passed through my teen years I found myself getting more and more sensitive to my surroundings. I began to smoke cigarettes to calm myself down and give me something else to focus on. But nothing soothed me. Somehow I made it through school and into college. However, in college I felt lost and finally got myself into counseling. My therapist recommended I take an Intuitive Development class. And I can say now, without reservation, that what I learned in that class saved my life.

Nothing in my upbringing or formal education told me about my energy body, or how to trust and use my intuition. I learned to listen to my body and soul's wisdom. I understood why I was so sensitive and what I could do about it. I understood about "being in my body" and how to use my psychic skills. I am in the process of quitting smoking as I share this story with you. I can honestly say that I am more myself *now.*

—Tammi, age 23

"Your soul grows sick with longing for the things it has forbidden itself."

—Oscar Wilde,
Irish poet and dramatist

The Invisible Hunter

from *Red Earth: Tales of the Micmacs*, by Marion Robertson

On the shores of a lake, near the village, lived an Invisible Hunter. Many strange tales were told about him, about his prowess as a hunter and how he looked, but no one ever saw him, no one could prove his tale. Many went to his wigwam and sat by his fire, and ate the food his sister gave them. They saw his moccasins when he drew them from his feet, and his coat when he hung it on a peg in the wigwam; but they never saw him. So many girls begged for a glimpse of him that he at last said he would marry the first one who could see him.

All the girls in the village flocked to his wigwam to try their luck. They were greeted kindly by his sister and invited to sit by the fire. In the evening she asked them to walk with her along the shores of the lake and, as they walked, she asked, "Do you see my brother on the farther shore?"

Some said that they did: others answered truthfully.

Those who said they could see him, she asked, "Of what is my brother's shoulder strap made?"

Some answered, "It is made from the skin of a young moose." Others said, "It is a whithe of the willow." Or, "It is a skin of beaver covered with shining wampum."

As they answered, she invited them back to the wigwam. When her brother entered the girls saw his moccasins when he dropped them on the floor of the wigwam; but they never saw him.

In the far end of the village lived three sisters who had the care of their father's wigwam. The two elder sisters were rough with the youngest, especially the eldest, who made her do all the heavy work and often beat her and pushed her into the fire. When they heard that the Invisible Hunter would marry the first girl who could see him, the two elder sisters hurried across the village to his wigwam. In the evening they walked along the shore of the lake, and the sister of the Invisible Hunter asked them, "Do you see my brother?"

The elder sister answered, "I can see him on the farther shore like a dark shadow among the trees."

The other sister said, "There are only trees on the farther shore."

The sister of the Invisible Hunter turned to the eldest sister and asked, "Of what is my brother's shoulder strap made?"

She answered lightly with a toss of her head.

"It is a strap of rawhide."

"Come then," said the sister of the Invisible Hunter, "let us hurry to the wigwam and cook food for my brother."

They hurried to the wigwam, and when the Invisible Hunter entered the sisters saw his moccasins and his hunting pack when he dropped them to the floor; but they could not see him.

"The rainbow is a sign from Him who is in all things."

—Hopi saying

"It is said that the advanced yogin, or bodhisattva, can leave this reality at will by changing the body's rate of vibration, transforming it into its subtle component of light and wind, known as the rainbow body."

—Peter Gold, author of *Navajo and Tibetan Sacred Wisdom*

The sisters went home pouting and were cross because they could not see the Invisible Hunter. When the youngest sister asked for some of the shells their father had brought to make wampum, the eldest sister slapped her and pushed her into the fire and shouted at her, "Why should any one as ugly and covered with scars and sores as you are want wampum?"

But the middle sister gave her a few shells and she made them into wampum and sewed them on an old pair of her father's moccasins. Then she went into the woods and gathered pieces of birch bark and made a dress, and with a charred stick she decorated it with the ancient symbols of her people. She made a cap and leggings, and, dressed in these and her father's moccasins and her dress of bark, she walked across the village to the wigwam of the Invisible Hunter. The Indians laughed and jeered, "Look at scars and sores going to the wigwam of the Invisible Hunter." But the sister of the Invisible Hunter greeted her kindly and invited her into the wigwam. In the evening she walked with her along the shores of the lake, and asked her as she had asked all the girls, "Do you see my brother?"

The girl answered, "Yes, I see your brother."

The sister asked again as she had asked all the others, "What is his shoulder strap made of?"

The girls answered, "His shoulder strap is a rainbow."

The sister of the Invisible Hunter laughed and drew the youngest sister back to the wigwam. She dressed her in soft skins, rubbed her scars with an oil that left her skin without blemish, and combed her stringy hair until it shone and was long and straight and black.

"Go, now, sit on my brother's side of the wigwam, nearest the door where the wife of the wigwam sits."

She who had been ugly and covered with scars sat in the place of the wife of the wigwam; and when the Invisible Hunter came, he sat beside her and made her his bride.

SEEING THE RAINBOW

Your body is the center of your life. Everything you know and feel comes from it or is experienced through it. So your relationship with your body will greatly determine what your life will be like. If you accept and care for your body, understand its language and energy, seek its wisdom, and feel the beauty that resides in it, you will live your life more fully.

To appreciate and be that attuned to your body you must nurture your Rainbow Body. Your Rainbow Body is part of, but more than, your physical body. It is your awareness of feelings and sensations. It is the intuitive understanding that you bring to those feelings and sensations. And it is the deep sense of your own innate beauty and truth. It is your Rainbow Body that puts you in touch with all the beauty, truth, and wonder around you.

This chapter will help you tap into that inner beauty and truth, that wisdom—through your Rainbow Body. Maybe you have felt like Tammi, detached from your body and confused by its signals. Maybe you can also recall a time when you really felt yourself *in* your body. Or, like the girl in the Micmac story, perhaps you can see what others cannot see—the Rainbow strap. You may even be the Invisible Hunter, waiting to be seen by your beloved.

Fortunately for all of us, no matter how things appear on the *outside* or how we may look to others (ugly, bruised, afraid), inside each of us lives great beauty and truth. In Navajo tradition there is a word for beauty: *hozhq.* It is used to describe the beauty of both men and women. Its meaning includes one's inner beauty. To be truly beautiful is to be in contact with your *inner* beauty and your Rainbow Body. Your sense of inner beauty is an important part of your intuitive self.

"**The seven colors of the rainbow represent an alternative to our binary black and white consciousness, offering us a world of multiple opportunities. The Rainbow Bridge expresses the diversity of light as it moves from source to manifestation. Its seven colors represent seven vibratory modalities of human existence, related to the seven chakras of Indian yogic tradition—energy centers that exist within each one of us.**"

—ANODEA JUDITH, PSYCHOLO-GIST, AUTHOR OF *EASTERN BODY, WESTERN MIND*

A Universal Symbol

The rainbow is universally seen as a symbol of a bridge between heaven and earth, as well as a place of passage. For many cultures it symbolizes a bridge between the supernatural and the natural worlds. In Genesis, the rainbow is a sign of God's presence and spiritual protection. The Buddha is said to have returned from heaven on a seven-colored staircase. Certain central African tribes believe that God uses the rainbow to show that s/he is trying to communicate with us. In ancient Greece, Iris, the Goddess of the Rainbow, was considered a messenger of the gods. The Japanese view the rainbow as a "floating bridge to heaven." In Tibetan Buddhism the Rainbow Body is the state of meditation when the body begins to be turned into pure light.

In so many cultures, rainbows are considered a form of divine speech, a way for us to communicate with heaven or the spirit world. Think of your Rainbow Body as your connection with heaven, with spirit, allowing you to draw upon the higher energies that are available to us all, that are *within* us all. Your Rainbow Body is your *entire* body, awakened, conscious, connected to your higher power, your inner beauty, and your strength. It is the physical body and the *energy* body. To awaken your Rainbow Body means to connect with something beautiful and powerful, within you and outside of you.

"Will you not open your heart to know What rainbows teach, and sunsets show?"

—RALPH WALDO EMERSON, AMERICAN WRITER AND NATURALIST

"Our Being is a brilliant pattern of energies: a spectrum of possibilities. The mystic discovers symbols . . . Symbols are windows through which we can view the Essential Nature of our Being."

—NGAKPA CHOGYAM, AUTHOR OF *RAINBOW OF LIBERATED ENERGY*

"Although we earth-surface walkers cannot travel on spider web-like bridges of rainbows and sunbeams from one plane to the next, or appear and disappear at will in our world, as do the Holy People, Navajo philosophers and Chanters tell us that *we can achieve their empowered state through our own efforts*. We can

develop our imperfect body minds to their potential state of beauty and everlasting life because *we are of the same stuff as the Holy People*. We are all emanations (to use a Buddhist term) of that oneness and power of Beauty permeating the feet, legs, body, mind and speech of the earth."

—PETER GOLD, AUTHOR OF *NAVAJO AND TIBETAN SACRED WISDOM: THE CIRCLE OF THE SPIRIT*

So no matter who you are, you too have a Rainbow Body. You too are made up of the same stuff as the Holy People.

AWAKENING YOUR RAINBOW BODY

Many things in this culture can separate you from your Rainbow Body. Physical and emotional abuse, too many "numbing out" activities, addiction to relationships, alcohol and drug abuse, too much focus on *doing* things rather than *being*, and worrying too much about how we appear to others—all of these things disconnect you from your Rainbow Body.

Waking up your Rainbow Body will result in many changes: You will:

- notice more about the people and things around you
- experience natural and positive "highs" (altered states)
- be more conscious, more aware, more present
- recognize more of your emotions
- be able to call upon positive and powerful emotional states
- be more creative and focused
- feel more independent and strong
- feel an increased sense of well-being over time

"Only those who risk going too far can possibly find out how far one can go."

—T. S. ELIOT, POET

"I know I walk in and out of several worlds every day."

—JAY HARJO, CREE INDIAN POET

I want to remind you that these exercises and states of consciousness—this awakening of the Rainbow Body, the Beauty Way (as it is called by the Navajo), *are what the ancients taught all their young people.* In fact, much of the wisdom within this book is a collection of practices borrowed from ancient cultures including Tibetan and Indian Buddhism, Japanese Zen Buddhism, Jewish mysticism, ancient Hinduism, Native American medicine, African tribal traditions, and ancient Toltec practice. *This information is intended for you.* It has always been intended for you.

Start with the Spine

The spine is the main highway of our energy. It is also in the spine that we will tend to develop blockages that prevent energy movement. That is why in many meditation practices we hold our spines comfortably upright, so this highway can be a straight and clear path for the energy to flow. In fact, we cannot successfully meditate, imagine, or think in a slouching position.

Try this once. Slouch over when you are trying to think, and notice how you feel in your body. What attitudes come along with this body posture? What feelings? How is your breathing in this posture? Now, sit upright, alert but not stiff. How does this feel in your body? What attitude accompanies this posture? How does it feel to sit upright? What is your breathing like? Not only do these postures affect your feelings, but they also send out a message to others. Thus, in all the meditations and exercises in the book (unless otherwise mentioned), sit in an upright, alert position, so the channel of your energy flow will be clear.

Grounding Meditation

For any of these exercises to work you must be "grounded" in your body. You must be able to have a conversation with your body and

"The colors of the heart center's rainbow light are the same colors as those of the cloth of (Tibetan) prayer flags and of the five primal elements of the cosmos (earth, water, fire, wind, and ether) out of which arise the body minds of all sentient beings."

—PETER GOLD, FROM *NAVAJO AND TIBETAN SACRED WISDOM*

its energy. The following grounding meditation was taught to me by my psychic and spiritual teacher, Colleen Brenzy, and it is the foundation for all the other exercises in this book.

I recommend that you practice this grounding meditation every day. Doing this meditation regularly will bring you more consciously into your body and it will begin awakening your Rainbow Body. After you have practiced it a few times, it will only take a minute or so to get grounded every day.

Sit in a chair, with your feet uncrossed and touching the floor. Gently close your eyes and bring your awareness to your breathing. Simply notice how your body feels without judgment; allow yourself to breathe naturally. Breathe . . . and notice the physical sensation of breath within your body, how it moves in and out and rises and falls in the belly. Continue to breathe while bringing your awareness down to the bottoms of your feet.

Now, continuing to breathe, imagine roots coming out from the bottoms of your feet. Visualize the roots reaching down through the floor and through the layers of the earth. Imagine this without forcing it . . . continue to breathe as the roots reach down deep into the earth, to its core. Now imagine the roots pulling up core earth energy, and that earth energy moving up through the roots. Still breathing, bring the earth energy up through the roots, into the bottoms of your feet, up through your legs, and into your abdomen, until it reaches your solar plexus, which is the area behind and around your belly button (also called the third chakra—see chapter 3). Fill this area up entirely with this core earth energy. Then imagine this energy moving back down and through the roots, into the earth. Envision this continual circle of earth energy coming in and going out. Sit for a few minutes in this grounded energy. Remember to breathe and to do this meditation with as little effort as possible. Trying

"When I was little I made a painting of a tree. It was going to be a landscape but I lost interest and now somewhere in the folio of my childhood drawings is one of a completed tree surrounded by white watercolor paper. I had completely forgotten the whole business.

"Then this morning I caught myself gazing at the tree I had once before 'seen' and painted, only now it was growing beside the driveway."

—LAWRENCE KUSHER, SPIRITUAL LEADER, AUTHOR OF *HONEY FROM THE ROCK: AN INTRODUCTION TO JEWISH MYSTICISM*

to force our visualizations only generates more stress. No need to force and push; just imagine and breathe . . .

If you ever find yourself scattered, afraid, or overwhelmed, grounding yourself will help. After practicing for a while you will find you can even become grounded with your eyes open (perhaps sitting in a classroom while the teacher is passing out the final exam!). Make certain to *breathe*, because your visualizations and meditations rely on your breathing. We tend to hold our breath or take shallow breaths when we are scared, and this just makes us more frozen in this negative fear energy. So, as the teacher is passing out the papers, instead of focusing on your worries, you can ground yourself—relax, focus, and breathe.

A Beauty Chant for Your Rainbow Body

Chanting and breathing were commonly used by the ancients to stimulate their well-being and awaken their spiritual natures. This chant is borrowed from the Navajo tradition. Similar chants or prayers are found in many other indigenous cultures. This chant can be a great daily morning prayer. Its simple yet powerful words will assist you in becoming stronger and more present in your body. It can also be sung or stated any time of the day as a reminder of the beauty that surrounds us all and is within each of us, all the time. I use it when I am feeling negative or "seeing" negativity all around me. It helps lift me up and gently brings me back to a more positive and strong place.

Beauty before me.
Beauty behind me.
Beauty below me.

"Grounding provides a connection that makes us feel safe, alive, centered in ourselves, and rooted in our environment."

—ANODEA JUDITH, PSYCHOLOGIST, AUTHOR OF *EASTERN BODY, WESTERN MIND*

"You are in this universe and this universe is in you."

—JAY HARJO, MUSKOGEE TRIBE POET AND MUSICIAN

Beauty above me.
Beauty beside me.
Beauty within me
I see beauty all around.
In beauty may I walk.
In beauty may I see.
In beauty may we all be.

"**When you are nervous, disoriented, or emotionally fragile, chanting or reciting a mantra inspiringly can change the state of your mind completely, by transforming its energy and atmosphere.**"
—SOGYAL RINPOCHE, TIBETAN LAMA, AUTHOR OF *TIBETAN BOOK OF LIVING AND DYING*

Lindy was a teen client of mine who was recovering from anorexia. She recited this chant every day for nearly a year. She describes its effect on her life: "The power of this chant reminded me of the truth about myself rather than the lies I had believed. You really can be beautiful *just as you are.* You don't have to change something to feel your beauty or potential." Having recovered from the anorexia and depression that she suffered in her teen years, Lindy has gone on to get a master's degree in yoga therapy. She is well *and* beautiful.

All chants have a similar intention—to connect us with our intuition and our energy body. Chanting and singing are said to massage the soul. That is why people in ancient cultures used chanting and singing to connect with the spirit world and with their own true nature. Chanting also encourages the chanter to breathe, and our body and soul love to breathe.

Chanting or saying empowering statements such as the Beauty Chant out loud as you focus on their meaning will help awaken your Rainbow Body. This is because they help you remember the *truth* about yourself. When you remind yourself that you have beauty and strength and wisdom inside, you connect your Rainbow Body to that positive energy, just like plugging an electrical appliance into an outlet.

Remember that the word *beauty* in this chant refers to inner beauty and applies to men as well as women. A young man named Jared decided to change the word *beauty* to *strength*. He found that saying this prayer before he went to bed at night helped him sleep: "It seemed to help protect me from the nightmares I had all the time. Before I learned the chant I felt a real dark presence enter my dreams. It was real creepy. Now, the chant seems to keep him away."

Sufi Breathing

Sufism is an ancient form of spiritual practice often thought of as the mystical arm of Islam, and it may be older than Islam, Judaism, and Christianity. Its main tenet is that God wants only for each of us to express our own true nature. According to Sufi belief, this true nature is always beautiful, and connected somehow to God. Although we may express it in many, many forms—as an artist, bus driver, teacher, musician—our true nature is always exquisite.

The following meditation uses the breath as a tool to connect with earth energy and to reach an altered state of consciousness. During this meditation you will be visualizing one thing as you breathe in, and something else as you breathe out. It will be helpful for you to read through the exercise a few times before you actually practice it. Or, you may want to record it or have it read out loud slowly by a friend or meditation teacher.

Begin by lying flat on your back on the earth (or on the floor), head to one side, ear flat to the ground (or supported by a pillow, as needed). As you inhale, imagine your umbilical cord extending down into the earth from

"The prophecies say that they would return as a rainbow people in bodies of different colors: red, white, yellow, and black. The old ones said that they would return and unite to help restore the balance to the earth."

—SUN BEAR, ELDER OF THE BEAR TRIBE

your belly button. Draw up energy from the earth through this cord, and let it enter your heart and heart chakra (see chapter 3). As your heart fills, allow the energy to spill over, filling your entire energetic Rainbow Body from head to toe. On the exhale, imagine all the negative energy—stress, negative thoughts, illness—flowing out your fingertips and toes back down into the earth, where it gets cleansed and recycled.

Visualize that on the inhale your heart and body fill up with earth energy, and on the exhale your body empties of all negativity. Let the exercise be as effortless as possible.

Make your breaths deeper and longer, with no gap between the in breath and the out breath. You will be breathing without pausing between the inhale and the exhale. This kind of breathing helps loosen up the negativity and send it out while at the same time making room for the more positive, mother earth energy to enter. (Earth energy in most spiritual traditions is considered regenerative; therefore, we can send our negativity into the earth to be recycled into positive energy.)

Repeat this breathing cycle ten times or for two minutes, synchronizing the bringing in of earth energy on the in breath and the releasing of all negative energy on the out breath. Remember not to pause between the in breath and the out breath.

You may feel a little "high" when you are finished. Enjoy this energy by giving yourself a couple of minutes to remain lying down. Bring your attention to the feelings and sensations within and around your body. Can you feel the Rainbow Body inside and outside your physical body? Do you notice how the sensations extend out past your physical body? This is your energy body.

"The energetic body is bigger than our physical body, which means that it includes parts that we normally do not see, such as the energy surrounding the physical body, which is known as the aura; feelings, and the dreaming body. Ultimately, the energetic body is the one that feels, the one that connects itself with what is out there."

—Victor Sanchez, author of *The Toltec Path of Recapitulation*

Body Awareness Meditation

The following meditation is borrowed from Buddhist mindfulness meditation practice. This meditation brings your awareness to the many sensations alive within your body. Typically, we move through a day oblivious to our body unless it is hungry or in pain. Chances are that there are parts of your body that go completely unnoticed until you purposefully bring your attention to them. It takes time and willingness to focus your attention, but the results are well worth it. I can remember doing this meditation and feeling my energy body for days afterward.

This meditation can take up to twenty minutes.

Have somebody read the following instructions out loud for you, or make a recording of them and play it when you're ready to meditate. Allow yourself plenty of time and a quiet place. This is a great meditation to do in a group.

Sit in a meditative posture, with your back in an upright, alert position. You can be sitting in a chair with your feet on the floor, or on a medita-

tion cushion. Just sit for a few breaths, in this body, bringing your aware-ness to the breathing, sitting body . . . Keep your awareness gently focused on the breathing body . . . Notice where you feel the breath in your body, letting the breath happen by itself.

Now bring your awareness down to your right foot and lower leg, and simply notice what sensations may be rising and falling there. Just notice, without judgment or preference . . . notice the sensations there . . . just breathe, and notice . . . breathe, and notice. Bring your attention now to your right thigh, noticing all the sensations that are rising and falling there . . . try not to react to these sensations (by scratching or shifting)—instead, just notice these physical sensations . . . and how they come and go in the body. Just notice . . .

Now bring your awareness to your left foot and lower leg, and notice what physical sensations are there . . . When you notice your awareness has moved elsewhere (to a thought), gently return your awareness back to the physical sensations in your left foot and leg . . . Just breathe, and notice . . . now moving your awareness up to your left thigh, notice the sensations that are there . . . notice what you feel in the front and back of your left thigh . . . breathing and keeping your awareness on the body . . .

Take your awareness now to your buttocks . . . notice the sensations there, perhaps the pressure of the cushion or chair against you . . . notice the sensations within your body there, below the skin . . .

Bring your awareness now to your sexual and reproductive organs, simply noticing what physical sensations are there . . . breathing and keeping your awareness on your sexual and reproductive organs . . . now moving your awareness to your midsection, the front and back and inside of your stomach and lower back . . . breathing in awareness of the sen-sations there . . . the tightening or loosening, the coldness or warmth that may be rising and falling there . . . feeling the breath making the belly rise and fall, rise and fall . . .

"The inherent Buddha-nature is said to be like a diamond, indestructible, pure and empty in itself, but luminous in reflecting the manifestation of ener-gies as rainbow light."

—TERRY CLIFFORD, AUTHOR OF *TIBETAN BUDDHIST MEDICINE AND PSYCHIATRY*

Now, moving your awareness to your chest and upper back, what sensations are there? . . . Notice how they change in intensity or shape . . . rising and falling, . . . coming and going . . . Now bring your awareness to your right hand and lower arm, noticing what sensations are there, as subtle as they may be or as intense as they may be . . . breathe and be aware of your body . . . Move up your right arm, bringing your awareness to your upper right arm and shoulder . . . breathe, noticing the physical sensations there . . . breathe and notice without judgment or reaction . . . just pure awareness . . . Now bring that awareness to your left hand and lower arm, noticing the physical sensations there . . . just breathe and notice . . . Now bring your awareness to your upper left arm and shoulder, sitting in pure awareness of this area of your body . . . just breathing in awareness . . . Now bring your awareness to your neck and throat area . . . breathing in and breathing out . . . with your gentle awareness lighting on the sensations that you feel in your neck and throat . . . breathing and maintaining an alert body . . . Now bring this awareness to your head, your ears, and the back and top of your head, and notice whatever sensations may be there . . . however strong or subtle they may be, noticing at times how they change . . . breathe and sit in this body . . . Now bring your awareness to your face, and all the muscles around your eyes and nose and mouth, noticing all the sensations on and inside your face . . . breathe and notice without judgment, just pure awareness . . .

Now sit in awareness of your breathing body . . . just pure and gentle awareness of your body sitting and breathing, . . .
sitting and breathing . . .
sitting and breathing . . .

Open your eyes slowly and take the time to notice what it feels like in this body that has been showered with so much awareness. You may want to share your experiences with the group or write them down in your journal. What does your body feel like now? What parts of your body did you visit for the first time? Were you able to notice some of your body's sensations without judgment? What was it like for you to bring so much pure, nonjudgmental awareness to your body?

HEALING THE ABUSED RAINBOW BODY

For some of you, being so present in your body may have been very emotional. This is often true for those of you who have experienced abuse or neglect. Neglect can come in many forms. Sometimes our families do not see who we truly are, or they are involved too much in their own lives to give us much attention. For some, neglect is the experience of *not* ever really being touched or loved.

Abuse also comes in many forms, which include emotional, psychological, psychic, and physical or sexual abuse. When someone belittles you or attempts to control or manipulate you, that is psychological abuse. Psychic abuse occurs when someone claims to know you better than you know yourself, and deliberately interferes with your thought process. Psychic abuse also happens on an energetic level when others invade your private space.

Our intuition speaks our truth, while abuse is motivated by lies. Most abusers justify their behavior by trying to find a way to somehow blame it on the abused. This justification is *a lie*. Nothing anyone does ever justifies abusing that person. If you have been abused, whatever the circumstances may have been, *the abuse is not your fault*. However, if you have been abused, it *is* up to you to heal from the abuse, to not let what someone else did to you destroy you. Each

"Each of us is surrounded by our own individual rainbow of colors."

—KENNETH MEADOWS, SHAMANIC HEALER AND AUTHOR OF *EARTH MEDICINE*

"All suffering is caused by the illusion of separateness, which generates fear and self-hatred, which eventually causes illness."

—BARBARA ANN BRENNAN, PSYCHIC HEALER, AUTHOR OF *HANDS OF LIGHT: A GUIDE TO HEALING THROUGH THE HUMAN ENERGY FIELD*

of us has the ability to rise up out of the most damaging situations. And it is during your teen and young adult years that you can begin this process of becoming free.

"In the dark time, the eye begins to see."

—THEODORE ROETHKE,
AMERICAN POET AND NATURALIST

"It always comes down to the same necessity; go deep enough and there is a bedrock of truth, however hard."

—MAY SARTON,
AMERICAN POET

"You are not responsible for his treating you like trash, but you are responsible for feeling like your life is ruined and having lived as though it is."

—VICTOR SANCHEZ, MEXICAN
HEALER, AUTHOR OF
*THE TOLTEC PATH
OF RECAPITULATION*

Neglect and abuse of the body can actually ignite our intuition. Tammi believed that "the abuses seemed to turn up my intuition. I had to trust *something* and that something was me. I realized that my 'sensitivity' was in many ways a response to the abuse." In the Indian story, the youngest girl was mistreated by her older sisters, and she was the one best able to see. When we are being "lied to" by the abuses of others (being told you are worthless is *always* a lie), we come to rely on a deeper, internal truth that we later discover is our intuition.

In addition to causing obvious physical and emotional damage, abuse and neglect cause *energetic* bruises and scars in your Rainbow Body. This harm to your energy body usually goes unnoticed, since most people in our culture aren't aware of this energy body even in its healthy state. The remaining exercises in this chapter can help your energy body heal from the harm that may have been done in the past. The wonderful thing is, when we heal the energy body, this results in emotional and physical healing as well. This is because our energy body is part of our physical body. (*Note:* If you are in a dangerous or abusive situation *now*, you can use the Psychic Protection exercises in chapter 5 to protect your Rainbow Body as you work to remove yourself from the abusive situation.)

Truths That Heal

To begin healing your Rainbow Body, you need to remember two truths:

- The world is a medley of possibilities for you.
- Each of us is born for a reason.

Believe and hold on to these truths about the world and yourself. If they don't *feel* true, it's only because you have been lied to for too long.

> *"In my senior year I attended a Seniors' Rites of Passage group. Before that I had no idea what I was going to do after I graduated. I was scared and stuck. I was an addict and was fighting to give up drugs. I didn't want to end up like my dad and uncle. They both smoked pot and worked in jobs they hated. Before this group it was hard to even imagine life beyond this place I grew up in. After doing a spiral meditation walk (see pages 164–169), a vision quest, and working with my dreams, I found a way out of this place. 'This place' was mostly inside me. I now know that life isn't against me . . . that even with a war going on, even with my dad stoned and unhappy, even with my mom afraid of me leaving, . . . there is a big world out there for me to discover. I have plans now. Plans that include moving away and living with some friends and attending a technical college. Plans that include something big—even though I am not entirely sure what that is."*
>
> —HENRY, AGE 18

How can such beliefs help you heal your energy body? Because what we *believe* to be possible—the thoughts we hold about ourselves and about the world—hold great power. Remember, *thoughts are energy.* As Steven Levine reminds us, "[T]he same energy that moves the clouds across the sky, moves our thoughts across our mind." The thoughts that I am referring to here are the ones that we hear in our heads *repeatedly*—the thoughts that we hold on to or that seem to hold on to us. Our habitual thoughts are really beliefs. These beliefs are much like prayers—a message that we send out to the universe, awaiting a response. The energetic messages we send out about ourselves and about the world tend to match up with like energy (similar energy) and then come back to us with even greater force.

For example, when someone sends out energy that says, "My life is shit, and there's no point . . .," you can imagine what he or she might get back. (Frankly, more shit.) Letting negative thoughts dominate your life can block out the positive things that are available to you. It is like going outside and looking up into the big blue sky and seeing one small gray cloud—and going back inside because you figure it's going to rain. If you have had bad luck and difficult circumstances for much of your life, it's natural to feel, to *believe*, that it will always be that way. However, when you hold on to such negativity, it is really difficult to actually *see* the possibilities when they *do* enter your life. And the fact is *good things are* always *trying to get into your life!*

The truth of that statement is illustrated by an experience I had when I was nineteen. I had applied for admission to the University of Wisconsin in Madison and I was not accepted. The woman at the admissions office said that my application was rejected because I didn't have enough algebra credits on my high school transcript. I left the building very upset and confused. Up until that point I had believed that I was meant to go to college, that I was meant to become a social worker and maybe even write a book some day. Now what was I going to do?

I left the admissions office discouraged but not hopeless. I sent out a prayer to Spirit. "What now?" I asked. I walked over to a local drugstore that had one of the last remaining soda fountains and ordered a Coke. As I sat at the counter, worried *but* also trying to consider my options, someone took the seat next to me.

And who do you think it was?

It was my high school algebra teacher! I told him about my situation, and he said that he would write a letter and set it straight with the university that I *had* taken enough algebra credits. Later that month I began my journey into higher education, ultimately going to graduate school and writing several books.

What if I had just gone home and given up? What if I was so bummed out that I didn't even look up from my Coke? And what if I had felt too hopeless to tell my algebra teacher what had just happened? You might say that, at that challenging time, I was able to see the "Rainbow strap"—and seize the moment. You might say that my *not giving up* helped Spirit put my algebra teacher on my path that day. You might say that, for each of us, good things are meant to be.

Can you carry with you some hope, even when life *appears* to be hopeless? Can you remain open to the very real opportunities that will show up on your path today and tomorrow? Can you be like the younger sister in "The Invisible Hunter"? Even though she was treated harshly by her family and her village, she followed her heart and believed in the possibility that something good could come into her life. If you can believe in possibilities, your Rainbow Body will help you to see them.

> *Sometimes I go about pitying myself,*
> *But all the while*
> *I am being carried by great winds*
> *across the sky . . .*
> —OJIBWE SONG

A Precious Human Life

"Every day, think as you wake up, today I am fortunate to have woken up.
I am alive, I have a precious Human Life, I am not going to waste it.
I am going to use all my energies to develop myself, to expand my heart out to others, to achieve Enlightenment for the benefit of all beings.
I am going to have kind thoughts towards others.
I am not going to get angry, or think badly about others as much as I can."

—PRAYER BY HIS HOLINESS THE 14TH DALAI LAMA

Ten Days That Can Change Your Life

When I wake up in the morning I begin the day with opening my heart and mind. Some days this is easy to do; on others days it can be a challenge. Before beginning my meditation and yoga practice, I remind myself of these truths: that *today* holds many possibilities and that there IS a reason for me to be alive, *today*. I suggest you try this for ten days. Before getting out of bed in the morning, say to yourself:

Today is full of possibilities for me. I am meant to be alive today—there is a greater purpose to my life.

Let the statements fill up your entire being. *Imagine* them as true. What might your life look like, feel like? What good might happen today? How would Spirit intervene in your life, *right now,* to help you out? How might your difficulty be changed into an opportunity? How would this change take place, what would it look like? Even though others may be discouraging or even abusing you, what can you choose to believe in anyway? Consider writing your responses to these questions in your journal.

If you notice that you have difficulty feeling these statements as real, *keep to it for ten days*. If you have been given the message over and over that things won't work out for you, you have been "programmed" to feel discouraged. If you have not been given concrete and real examples of the wonderful possibilities waiting for you, then it will be hard for you to imagine them. It can take a while to change this negative tape—this *lie*—to a truth. But give it time. If you miss a day, try starting over until you can do the statements for ten days in a row.

Remember to *imagine* these beliefs to be true when you say them in the morning. Send out that thought, that prayer, to the universe for ten days. *Mark the ten days* on a calendar and notice what internal and external changes occur in your life as you begin each day with these affirmations. What good has come into your life during these ten days? If you'd like to, e-mail me at Jewelhrt8@aol.com and tell me what has changed in your life.

Telling Your Story

A powerful tool that the ancients used to heal and strengthen the Rainbow Body was to tell their story to the elders in their community. Sharing your story with a therapist, trusted healer, or elder can help you heal from abuse. Have you ever noticed how sharing something painful with a trusted friend just *feels* better? Telling your story helps move any negative energy out of your Rainbow Body, so it is no longer carrying your secret and your pain.

The healing power of story includes the ability to help the one hearing the story as well. You will find that certain stories in this book have a healing effect on you. Notice the ones that resonate with you. In what ways are they like your own story? What gets stirred up as you read the stories of other teens? Which ancient stories feel as if they were written for you? Answering these questions can help you tell your own story.

Write It Out

Sometimes, *writing it out* is a way to release the pain from your body. The physical and emotional process of writing through your pain moves the negative energy out from the Rainbow Body, so you don't have to carry it inside you. To write out your thoughts and feelings is also a way for you to discover your truth, to be honest with yourself. Remember to write for yourself, not for someone else's approval.

You may want to begin by answering some of the following questions in your journal.

1. Which characters in "The Invisible Hunter" do you identify with?

Often we will identify with more than one character. I identify with both the Invisible Hunter and the middle sister. Like the hunter, I felt invisible because my family never acknowledged my

". . . Facts can obscure the truth."
—MAYA ANGELOU,
POET, PLAYWRIGHT,
AND SOCIAL ACTIVIST

"The world is made up of stories, not of atoms."
–MURIEL RUKEYSER,
POET AND SOCIAL ACTIVIST

"beauty." I was also honest like the middle sister (she said she didn't see the Invisible Hunter). I believe my honesty is one of my better qualities. Later in my life, I became like the youngest sister, recovering from the bruises and scars of my childhood and able to "see" the rainbow in myself and in others. Now, I consider myself the sister of the Invisible Hunter, helping young men and women find their own true nature. Who you identify with is likely to change with time as well.

2. What exercises in this chapter helped you feel your Rainbow Body? What did it feel like?

"I could feel my energy go out from my body—I could feel myself extend out past my skin. The breathing exercise is way powerful."

—ANNE, AGE 17

3. What belief, if any, has changed for you as a result of reading this far into the book and practicing some of the exercises?

Your Rainbow Body is waking up, Now you are ready to move on to the next chapter and learn about the body's energy centers, the chakras.

"We have been taught to believe that negative equals realistic and positive equals unrealistic."

—SUSAN JEFFERS,
PSYCHOLOGIST AND AUTHOR

"The future enters into us in order to transform us, long before it happens."

—RAINER MARIA RILKE,
GERMAN POET

I thank you God for this most amazing
day: for the leaping greenly spirits of trees
and a blue true dream of sky; and for everything
which is natural which is infinite which is yes.

—E. E. CUMMINGS, AMERICAN POET

"You are not inside your body, your body is inside you."

—W. Brugh Joy, M.D.,
SPIRITUAL TRANSFORMATION TEACHER

3

The Chakras
Your Seven Centers of Power

◎ VAMPIRE ENERGY: JARED'S STORY ◎

Jared was a young man whose family moved around a lot. He had a hard time fitting in, and found himself rejecting most of the high school experience. He came to me suffering from many illnesses, including depression. He said he had curvature of the spine, chronic throat problems, jaw and tooth problems, multiple allergies, thyroid problems, and that he suffered from nightmares and sleeplessness. (All these illnesses are related to the fourth chakra, which is described later in this chapter.) The odd thing was, he didn't appear sick.

He had a history of difficult relationships, depression, and abuse. His energy was depleted, weak and vulnerable to negative influences. His entire energy body was depressed. Up until then he was being treated with traditional healing medicines only, and he had not been introduced to such complementary practices as yoga, acupuncture, and energy work. The energy damage that he had experienced had not been acknowledged. This is not to say that his medical problems weren't real (they were) but that the damage to his energy body clearly needed attention. Meanwhile, he had become deeply involved in the vampire "religion,"

"**As guardian of myster-
ies, snake implies the
workings of divine
energy through one's
life. As an introduction to
sacred knowledge, snake
supplies support for
transformation at the
deepest levels.
Remember though,
this process is probably
best represented by the
double-edged sword, for
snake also suggests lying
and deceit.**

**Its energy is destruc-
tive as well as fruitful.
The slippery nature of
snake energy requires
cautious handling, for it
can be used for good as
well as ill. The most positive application of snake
energy is to deepen one's
understanding.**"

—JESSICA DAWN PALMER,
AUTHOR OF *ANIMAL WISDOM:
THE DEFINITIVE GUIDE TO
THE MYTH, FOLKLORE
AND MEDICINE POWER
OF ANIMALS*

which promotes the sucking of other people's energy as a way to increase one's own power.

In my work with Jared we focused on tapping his own energy and using it in a more positive and creative way. I helped him understand that he had plenty of his own power and energy to access and use; he didn't need to suck anyone else's. (I also pointed out that while it is possible to feed off someone else's energy, it is not possible to actually put that hijacked energy to use, as the vampire religion claims, which is one reason those who succeed at sucking your energy need to keep doing it.)

I taught Jared the chakra meditations in this chapter, and he learned how to tap the vast resources of his own energy body. He began consulting the I Ching for Teens to help develop his intuitive skills. He is now able to sleep without nightmares and holds a more positive outlook on his life. He consults the I Ching regularly and is practicing and enjoying more positive uses of his energy.

HOW SNAKE GOT ITS MEDICINE
adapted by Julie Tallard Johnson from a traditional South American story

Long, long, long ago, before there were clocks or watches, when creatures would tell time only by the moon, all the birds lived in the Great First Forest. At that time all the birds were black, or white, or black and white. In the First Forest there also lived a great, big, green snake. One morning, as he slithered along, the snake noticed some red flowers. Without much thought or effort, he went and ate them all. As he glided on, the snake caught sight of his tail and turned his head to have a better look. Along his body were circles of red. "Strange," thought the snake, "but nice, very nice."

Later, the snake came to some orange flowers. And without much thought or effort, he ate them all too. Then he turned his head to look at his body. Yes, bright orange circles were beginning to appear. The snake *was delighted. He was surely the most colorful creature in the land. He wound his way through the forest, eating up the yellow flowers, then the bright green ones, then the ones that were the color of the sky, then all the ones which were indigo and finally all the purple flowers. He did this all without much thought or effort.*

By the end of the day, his skin had circles of red, orange, yellow, green, blue, indigo, and purple on it. "I am a most beautiful snake," he hissed, coiling around so he could admire all of his body. And his entire body did shimmer like a beautiful rainbow.

But the birds of the First Forest were angry. They gathered around the snake, whistling, singing, and chirping. "Look what you've done!" they cried. "You've eaten all of the flowers and spoiled the forest. It is only green now."

The snake looked around him, and he knew that the birds were right. He felt bad for eating up all the flowers for himself. He crept away to a dark corner. There, he shook, and shook, until suddenly, his skin began to split. Slowly he wriggled out of it and glided across the forest floor in a new green skin, leaving a bright rainbow skin behind. He looked at his own green skin, and realized for the first time how beautiful it was, and how perfect it was for his stealthy travels through the forest.

The birds soon found the rainbow skin. Without much thought or effort they tore it up with their beaks, and draped pieces of it over their bodies and wings. Soon their feathers turned the colors of red, blue, orange, yellow, purple, and indigo. Each bird got a piece, because in the Beginning Times every creature knew that there is always enough to go around.

The snake slithered off happily, green once again, and the birds flew away and sang new songs, showing off their beautiful colors.

And the Great Forest was green and ready for new growth again.

Jared and the snake both thought that they had to "gobble up" power from outside themselves. But true power is personal power—the power within ourselves. Personal power is a positive force we create inside us,

"Everything an Indian
does is in a circle, and
that is because the Power
of the World is in circles,
and everything tries to
be round . . . The sky is
round and I have heard
that the earth is round
like a ball and so are all
the stars. The wind, in its
power, whirls. Birds make
their nests in circles, for
theirs is the same reli-
gion as ours. The sun
comes forth and goes
down again in a circle.
The moon does the same,
and both are round. Even
the seasons form a great
circle in their changing,
and always come back
again to where they
were. The life of man is
a circle from childhood
to childhood, and so it
is in everything where
power moves."
—BLACK ELK,
OGLALA SIOUX ELDER

not something we get from others or use to control others. We all have this power. Native Americans refer to this personal power as one's "medicine." All living things have medicine. How you come to understand and use this power, this medicine inside of you and around you, will determine what kind of person you become. How do you experience your power, your medicine so far? Are you empowered with high self-esteem and hope or do you have a power deficit—a sense of powerlessness and hopelessness? Fortunately, every one of us can harness power and energy from within and use it in a life-fulfilling way.

YOUR SEVEN CHAKRAS

Within each of us are seven specific centers of energy and power. In yoga philosophy, these centers are referred to as *chakras,* which literally means "wheels" or "disks." The chakras are part of our Rainbow Body, power centers that hold and release energy. You could say they

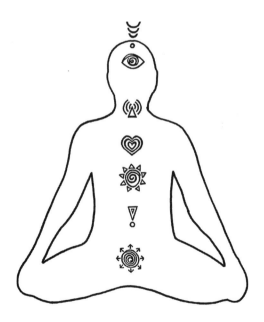

are wheels of energy, with each chakra generating a specific kind of power. These energy centers hold vital information about your body, your soul, and your mind. They even hold information about your relationships and environment.

Your seven major chakras are stacked in a row beginning at the base of your spine and ending at the top of your head (see drawing on page 58). Chakras are not physical objects that you can touch with your hands; they are sources of energy. The energy generated from these chakras is similar to other forms of energy such as wind, electricity, and heat. We know it is there because it has an effect on us, but it is not something we can see or hold.

"Just as we see the wind through movement of the leaves and branches, the chakras can be seen by what we create around us."
—JUDITH ANODEA, PSYCHOLOGIST,
AUTHOR OF *EASTERN BODY, WESTERN MIND*

Knowledge and use of the chakras is based on a system of medicine and philosophy that originated in India over four thousand years ago. When you find that you have some difficulty with either your health or your personal life, the chakras can help you understand what might be out of balance and how you can heal the problem energetically.

The chakras develop sequentially, like other parts of our body and spirit. As teenagers and young adults you are developing and activating your sixth chakra, or third eye. Your interest in spiritual matters and symbolism, which are elements of the sixth chakra, peaks during this time of your life. As you already know, this is also a time when you are rethinking and defining who you are. For this reason, I will give extra attention to the sixth chakra in this chapter and in chapter 7.

How to Work with the Chakras

This chapter will introduce you to each of the chakras and explain the particular aspect of your life that each one influences. It will also identify issues and symptoms related to blocked or out-of-balance chakras, and offer exercises and meditations to strengthen and balance them. You will also learn how to balance your chakras using affirmations, color, flower essences, medicinal stones, and nature's medicine. Such attention to the chakras will result in better overall health of your mind, body, and spirit.

Affirmations

Affirmations are used to strengthen the chakra and to eliminate the lie that you may have come to carry in that chakra. The lie for the first chakra, the chakra of belonging, would be "I do not belong." So the affirmation is "I have a right to be here." Such an affirmation works best when you take a moment to feel the truth of the statement . . . let it seep into your entire being.

The Power of Affirmations

The words of an affirmation alone don't hold much power—it is the use of our imagination along with the affirmation that makes it real. Take some time with a given affirmation to truly imagine what it would be like for that statement to be 100 percent true for you. "I have a right to be here . . ." How would you feel, act, and look when this affirmation was true? What would your relationships look like? What emotions would you experience? Notice what it is like in your body and environment when this affirmation feels true for you.

Colors for Balancing the Chakras

As with all other aspects of the energy body, the chakras are understood and experienced energetically. We "see" the colors of the chakras intuitively. Chakras contain many colors, but each chakra is associated with a primary color—its color when it is in its best condition. We can use the primary color as a way to help heal and balance the chakra, by bringing it into our environment or our thoughts. For example, if you have a third chakra that is out of balance, you will want to visualize its primary color, bright yellow, to help you to bring this chakra into balance. Or you might want to wear red on a day you want to activate the first chakra. You will notice that I included an image of red soil in the healing meditation for the first chakra.

Bach Flower Remedies

Bach Flower Essences are thirty-eight homeopathically prepared flower essences discovered by Dr. Edward Bach in the 1930s. "Homeopathic" remedies are always gentle, with small amounts of a natural ingredient to help you heal. They will not interfere with any medication you may be taking. The Bach Flower Essences are part of a system of healing directed at the personality, mood, and emotional outlook of the individual receiving treatment. Dr. Bach believed that "disharmony with oneself is the root of all disease." And for this reason he created these remedies to heal and bring harmony to the body, mind, and spirit.

These and other flower remedies may be found at your local health food store.

Using Stones to Heal and Balance

The energy of certain semiprecious stones and minerals can be used to enhance or offset the energy in the chakras. In ancient times people

"The impact of the remedies [Bach Flower Essences] is reflected in shifts of attitude, emotional well-being, lifestyle, and even various physiological responses, as change which is introduced in nonphysical realms filters through to bodily consciousness."

—*FLOWER ESSENCE REPERTORY,* THE FLOWER ESSENCE SOCIETY

Gray coyote stood in the forest,
From his shoulders he plucked feathers
That gave me shining power,
Plucked wing feathers bearing power."
—PIMA SONG, FROM *SHARED SPIRITS: WILDLIFE AND NATIVE AMERICANS*, DENNIS L. OLSON

were in regular contact with such natural objects, since they lived closer to the earth. To heal our environments, our bodies, and our relationships, traditional spiritual practices suggest we come in contact with the natural properties of stones and plants. Everything has energy—and the energetic properties of stones are ancient (they have been around for a very long time).

Hold a stone in your hand or place it over the given chakra, then bring your awareness to that chakra. Imagine the energy of the stone filling up this chakra. Simply breathe and relax. With little effort, just imagine the medicinal properties and energies of the stone reaching and filling the chakra. Allow yourself to drift off in a daydream, or sleep . . . allowing the energy of the stone to heal and strengthen you on its own.

Have you found yourself attracted to a certain kind of stone? It would be worth your while to look up the healing properties of that particular stone. You are likely choosing it intuitively.

If a particular chakra is out of balance or needs more attention, you may want to keep one or more of the related stones in your bedroom. Many healers place stones under chairs, as well as in the corners of the rooms where they do healing work on others. You will find these stones at spiritually oriented shops, as well as rock shops and bead stores.

The Chakra Elements

Each chakra represents and shares the qualities of an element such as earth, water, or air. The work of many healing professionals including acupuncturists, shamanic healers, Tibetan doctors, and shiatzu practitioners involves diagnosing which elements are out of balance within your energy body. For each of the chakras, I will describe a medicine from the natural world that will help bring its particular element into balance.

Locating the Chakras

To find a chakra, simply sit in an upright position in a chair with your feet on the floor. Then, close your eyes and take a couple of deep breaths.

Do the grounding meditation you learned in chapter 2, and keep breathing . . . Now, with your inner vision (your imagination), go to the location of the chakra you want to focus on. For example, go to the base of the spine for the first chakra or to the spot above and between your eyebrows for the sixth chakra. Practice simply noticing what is there . . . try not to hold any expectations or assumptions about what you should find. Breathe as you look and notice the colors you might see, the sensations you might feel, the images that may appear. Breathe . . . and notice. When you are finished, slowly open your eyes and then journal about what you experienced.

In this exercise, you are visiting the chakras without any intention of balancing them; you are simply learning how to find a given chakra. Take the time to locate every chakra until you can easily go to that location without much effort.

First Chakra: The Chakra of Belonging

The first chakra is located at the base of the spine near the tailbone. It is also called the root or base chakra.

The first chakra deals with our sense of safety and belonging, security, and groundedness. It holds the energy that motivates you to take care of yourself. When this chakra is in good shape, you are eating and sleeping well and not taking dangerous risks. (You are, however, taking healthy risks!) The energy of this chakra is important in keeping you alive and out of danger. So, when you are feeling afraid, anxious, and separate from the world around you, this is the chakra that needs your attention. Chances are that in your teen years this chakra is overactive or stressed. A continually overactive first chakra can contribute to addictions such as drug abuse and even compulsive gambling.

Symptoms of an underactive first chakra include depression, anorexia, chronic fatigue, too much daydreaming and fantasizing, and addiction to nicotine. Symptoms of an overactive first chakra include overeating (to calm oneself down or to substitute for a sense of belonging), gambling, alcohol and drug abuse, and self-mutilation.

The primary emotional issue of this chakra is fear. This means that the energy of fear gets stuck in or originates from this chakra. So, if you are feeling fearful about something or experience panic attacks, focus on healing and strengthening this chakra. This includes getting medical attention for any physical issues in this chakra.

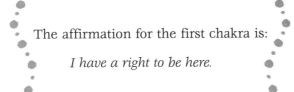

The affirmation for the first chakra is:

I have a right to be here.

Healing Meditation for the First Chakra

The grounding meditation on page 37 will be helpful here. Once you have grounded, bring your awareness to this chakra and begin to imagine planting a sacred garden there. Imagine planting seeds that will sprout up with all the people, symbols, animals, and objects that bring you a feeling of well-being and support. Plant your seeds in the red-rich soil of this chakra and see the images bloom. Feel yourself rich in the support of all these people, animals, and objects that nurture you . . .

Breathe and enjoy the richness of this garden. Think of it as your sacred tribal garden—all these people, animals, and objects make up your tribe. Be sure to include an ancestor who may have passed, such as a grandparent, who would bring strength and beauty to your garden. If people or objects are appearing that are not supportive, remove them as you would a weed, roots and all—then place them in an imaginary compost bin and shut the lid tightly. Savor the strength and the richness of your beautiful sacred garden.

Being in healthy relationships where you feel supported will always be a way to improve the condition of the first chakra. Close, healthy friendships are essential to your mental, physical, and spiritual health.

- The color of this chakra is red or reddish orange.
- The Bach Flower remedies for this chakra are Sunflower and Corn.
- A stone to help heal and strengthen the first chakra is black tourmaline. This mineral is special to many American Indian tribes. It can be used to ground the first chakra with the earth. It holds many protective qualities, which include blocking off the negative energy of others.
- The element of this chakra is earth.

Medicine from the Natural World

For this first chakra, you will be connected with the energy of earth (which is why grounding is such a great practice for this chakra, as is the above sacred tribal garden meditation).

Spend some time under a tree, or go for a nice slow walk outside—away from the noises of the city, if possible. Find and touch a small rock or carry one with you (a black tourmaline would be ideal). Walk barefoot on the ground. Basically, spend some time touching the earth.

"Grounding and anchoring work at the physical level, with some good deep breaths into the belly, is essential before any psychic work is undertaken."

—JUDY HALL,
PSYCHIC HEALER

SECOND CHAKRA:
THE CHAKRA OF SEXUALITY

This chakra is located below your navel and above the genitals. It is often called the body chakra because it is where you connect with the physical body through your senses. The second chakra is the chakra of sensuality, sexuality, and pleasure. It is also the chakra of emotions. From this chakra you are able to tune into others emotionally. When it is unblocked, this chakra allows for the free flow of your emotional, sensual, and creative energy throughout your body. It is through our feelings and our senses (touch, taste, smell, sight, and hearing) that we feel and interact with the world around us. Without a clear connection to your senses, you may have a "numbness" in your body and difficulty interpreting (understanding) your environment.

In our culture we are often taught to repress our natural pleasure states. We are not supposed to be emotional in public, and we are not to exhibit too much pleasure or energy at school. Often, adults in our culture are uncomfortable with teenagers coming into their own sexual energies. Because of these cultural attitudes, to "be good" and "behave" can often translate into shutting down and denying some of your important senses.

When basic pleasures are denied, such as your healthy sexuality, emotional expression, and sensual curiosity, you may find yourself choosing substitute "pleasures" such as drugs, drinking, video games, television, and overeating. You may also resort to negative behaviors including avoiding responsibility, blaming others for your troubles, and sexually acting out. Because˄ substitute pleasures are not truly fulfilling, you find yourself having to keep doing them again and again. It's like eating one marshmallow when what you really crave is a big fresh strawberry sundae. Anodea Judith, author of *Eastern Body, Western Mind,* sums it up nicely: "Healthy pleasure brings satisfaction; addictive pleasure brings a craving for more." This is a time to explore healthy ways to be a sensual, feeling individual.

Sexual energy is a sacred, vital, and intimate energy that connects us to someone else in a very special way. Sexual energy flows through everything that is alive. In the springtime we can see this energy come alive in animal and plant life.

Discovering your sexual energy in your teen years is part of claim-

"E-motions are energy in motion. If they are not expressed, the energy is repressed. As energy it has to go somewhere. Emotional energy moves us as does all energy . . . To deny emotion is to deny the ground and vital energy of our life."
—JOHN BRADSHAW, AUTHOR, COUNSELOR, TALKSHOW HOST

"Balance (in the second chakra) involves the ability to nurture self and others while still maintaining healthy sexual and emotional boundaries."
—ANODEA JUDITH, AUTHOR OF *EASTERN BODY, WESTERN MIND*

ing and opening the second chakra. This does not necessarily mean having sex (although it can). It does mean feeling your sexuality and your sensuality as a vital and sacred part of your humanness. It includes enjoying the scent of someone's cologne, the touch of a friend, the taste of your favorite food, the feel of tears on your cheek, the sound of a really good laugh, and the stunning colors of autumn leaves.

Healthy expression of your sexual energy may mean simply enjoying the way your body heats up when you think about or stand near a particular person. When you value and find real pleasure in your sexuality, you won't need to get caught up in substitute pleasures. Be very conscious of how you use this energy and whom you choose to share it with. Honor it as the sacred energy that it is. If you choose to be sexual with someone, be conscious about the reasons for your choice, and be realistic about what you can expect from that shift in your relationship.

◉ TARA'S STORY ◉

Tara was only fourteen when she was overheard in study hall saying she was "giving boys blow jobs at the party on Saturday." The nurse at the school was asked to talk with her. She asked Tara, "What were your reasons for doing this, and what did you want from it?" Tara told the nurse that she did it because she was "curious" and had heard that others did it. Then she had bragged about it because she thought other kids might think she was cool.

The nurse explained some basics to Tara—for instance, the fact that you can get transmittable diseases, some of them fatal, through oral sex (because it is an exchange of mucus). She asked Tara to think about the idea that each time we have sex with someone we give part of ourselves to this person, and if we do this all through our high school years, how much of ourselves will be left? The nurse asked her to think about how she will feel when this boy ignores her or when she sees him flirting with another girl. And then she asked Tara how she had felt when she was casually having oral sex with a boy. Tara couldn't actually recall feeling anything—she said she was pretty numb and was just "doing it." At age fourteen, Tara was already giving herself away and shutting down from her precious sensual body.

Both the boys and the girl in this situation gave vital energy away. They were not treating the sexual interaction as sacred, and were treating each other as objects. The energy body knows when it is being treated carelessly. Such an experience leaves scars on the Rainbow Body, and drains vital energy.

The affirmations for the second chakra are:

I have a right to feel and have pleasure.
My sexuality is sacred.

- The color of this chakra is orange.
- The Bach Flower remedies for this chakra are Larch, Sweet pea, and Pomegranate. You can blend all three together or use just one.
- Stones to help heal the second chakra are obsidian and black tourmaline. Obsidian is volcanic glass. It is another grounding and protective stone. Because it holds stabilizing energies, helping balance and protect you emotionally, it is a good stone for anyone who has been emotionally or otherwise abused. Many shamanic traditions use black obsidian in healing ceremonies to help in the removal of a disease from the body. The healer takes the obsidian to the wound, visually brings the illness outside the body, and transforms it into white light.
- The element of this chakra is water.

Medicine from the Natural World

Find a clean, moving body of water such as a river, stream, or creek. If it is warm enough, sit in the moving water and let it flow over you. If you choose a river, make sure you can sit in the water without having to fight the current. If the weather is too cold to get in the water, simply sit next to a body of moving water, and listen to the movement of the water.

A Healing Exercise for the Second Chakra

Try using this Japanese pressure point treatment to move the energy throughout your body and to awaken the senses. Bring the thumb and index finger together. Find the tender spot located on the hump formed by joining the two fingers, as shown above. Press it gently with your other thumb and breathe. Make sure to take several deep breaths while you press. This treatment will help move blocked sexual energy, and give you a sense of relaxation. This also helps release stuck energy throughout the entire energy body. Give yourself several daily treatments for a week for the best results.

Healing Meditation for the Second Chakra

Notice (or imagine) the water moving around you . . . notice how this feels. Allow this movement of water to remind you that you too are like water . . . moving, changing, strong yet fluid . . . Allow all the senses to awaken to the flow of the water . . . Let it carry away anything that is ready to leave you, such as negative thoughts, depression, worries, addictions . . . let the water baptize you in its powerful medicine. Allow as much time as possible for this—at least fifteen minutes. Let the water awaken your sensations and pleasures.

Imagine it moving through you . . . and around you, carrying away your worries and bathing you in its pleasures and powers.

If you have been sexually abused, Myron Eshowsky, a shamanic healer from North America, recommends that in addition to therapy (psychotherapy, massage therapy) you find a way to "bathe in the earth." You can do this by burying your lower torso (from your belly button down) in the sand or in the earth. Dig a hole in the sand or dirt and cover up your bare legs and stomach with the earth. (If you have access to a safe, private place, doing this unclothed would be ideal.)

Ask that the healing properties of the earth absorb the pain and trauma from your body. Imagine that the earth is taking away all the pain and abuse, while your sexual and reproductive organs are getting renewed. Rest there for about five minutes and let the natural and spontaneous healing properties of the earth heal you.

Third Chakra:
The Chakra of Personal Power and Independence

The location of this chakra is the solar plexus, above the navel. It is the location where you have been bringing in the earth energy from the grounding meditation. This chakra holds the energy of your willpower, independence, and decision making. The body's energy is generated from the third chakra.

Here, too, is where the energy of personal power is generated. If you feel sluggish, tired, and slowed down, your third chakra may need some healing attention. If your personal power seems bankrupt, this is the chakra to focus on. During your teen years this chakra is dominant because you are coming into your personal power. This means that every day your third chakra is being prodded. Every day you are dealing with issues of individuality—concerns of the third chakra.

When this chakra is balanced you have strong self-esteem, you feel confident, and you have a sense of your own personal power—you can confidently take responsibility for your own actions and their consequences. This is the chakra that generates healthy risk taking. A well-balanced third chakra will enable you to handle the challenges that the teen years are constantly bringing you.

When this chakra is out of balance because you do not have enough energy here, you can feel tired, be easily manipulated or confused by others, have low self-esteem, feel cold in your body, and you may be addicted to stimulants (caffeine, speed, cocaine). In addition, you may tend to blame others for your difficulties, and have a tendency not to be reliable.

An imbalance due to too much energy in this chakra can manifest as aggressive, domineering, arrogant, and stubborn behavior. Other signs of this imbalance are a tendency to be dishonest with others and being overly competitive (instead of simply wanting to do your best, you want to always be the best). You may also be addicted to sedatives (alcohol, downers).

Exercising Your Personal Power

Just what does it mean to have personal power? To exercise your personal power is to become the cause of your life rather than the effect of your life. Personal power is knowing that your life is a series of choices, and that your life happens in direct response to the choices you make.

This means that you don't blame others for what happens in your life and how you handle it. Personal power is an expression of your independence and autonomy. If you blame others for what troubles you, or for your inability to change, then you are powerless. Life becomes something that happens to you; you are life's victim. Empowering yourself, taking responsibility for your life, makes you the cause of your life. You become life's cocreator, along with whatever your higher power may be.

Life then becomes a journey with you in the driver's seat, your spiritual support behind you. Of course, you cannot prevent some bad things from happening to you or to those you care about. It is in your response to these challenges that you will find your personal power and independence. You have the power to decide how you will respond to circumstances, even though you may not have chosen the circumstances.

"All things have inner meaning and form and power."
—HOPI SAYING

The way to respond to negative events is to focus on maintaining your personal power by not letting anything make you shrink, by not letting any situation get "bigger" than you. When you become overwhelmed, take the actions of others too personally, or feel ganged up on, you have given up your personal power. You have let the emotion or event get bigger than you.

Even when someone in authority is lecturing or reprimanding you, you can still remain empowered as you listen to his or her point. You never have to shrink or feel small. (Those in authority should not act in ways that encourage you to shrink or lose your personal power. But we all know people who use their authority in this negative way.)

Being empowered personally means to always remember the truth about yourself. When you are true to yourself, no person or event can really diminish you.

Your Spiritual Source

Your higher power, or spiritual source, may be simply the great Tao—that invisible, mysterious energy that connects us all. Or you may be a cocreator with nature, tuning in to the natural rhythms of life. I connect up with what is referred to as the Great Mystery—a spiritual source that is bigger than I am, but is also within me and within all things. So much of it is a mystery to me, yet I feel its power and love in my life, especially when I call upon it. I also know that when I take responsibility for my life, this spiritual source does its part in supporting me. Trust that when you take responsibility for your journey, you are connecting up with this Great Mystery.

Giving Up Personal Power: The Comparing Game

Our biggest mistakes in our lives are typically due to a loss of personal power and autonomy. One of the most common ways teenagers (and people of all ages) short-circuit their personal power is by comparing themselves to others. If you compare yourself to others and you see yourself as "less than," you will feel bad about yourself and feel separated from the people you aspire to be like. When you compare yourself and you feel "better than," you risk becoming arrogant and again separating yourself from others. Comparison always results in a loss of personal power.

Think back on a time when you compared yourself to someone else. What did it feel like? Could you feel your personal power being drained from you? Could you feel the negative energy involved in comparing yourself to other people?

> *"I remember attending a spiritual retreat for teens when I was sixteen. I didn't feel I belonged there but I went because a friend of mine wanted me to go. All I could do for the first few days was compare myself to everyone around me. First everyone else was a geek or too fat, or too something . . . or not enough of something else. Then, into the third day everyone somehow became better than me and I felt awful. I wanted to leave. Finally, on the morning of the last day of the retreat, the leaders led us through a meditation where we all experienced our sameness [see Loving-kindness meditation on page 208]. It was about letting go of judging others and myself, and letting go of comparing myself to others. It was a huge relief not to compare myself to everybody else. It is hard not to do. But I am trying to see everyone without comparing myself to them."*
>
> —KAYLA, AGE 19

"As we develop a sense of self, our intuitive voice becomes our natural and constant source of guidance."

—CAROLINE MYSS,
MEDICAL INTUITIVE

"Empty inside, our cultural myth tells us that power lies outside of ourselves in the approval of others, in technological gadgets, or through a distant and authoritarian god. Thus we deplete ourselves, our resources, and our planet, reaching for a power outside, a power over, a power that will only enslave us."

—ANODEA JUDITH, *EASTERN BODY, WESTERN MIND*

The affirmations for the third chakra are:

The fire within me burns strong and I feel my independence.
I feel the power that is within me. I act from this center of power.

- The color of this chakra is bright yellow.
- The Bach Flower remedies for this chakra are Buttercup and Goldenrod.
- A stone to help heal the third chakra is jasper.
- Jasper is a form of opaque stone, and appears in a wide range of colors. It is often worn by shamans for protection. Its energy is connected to the solar plexus and worn to protect the third chakra, especially when journeying (see chapter 7).
- The element of the third chakra is fire.

Your Power Profile

For one week, really explore this idea of personal power. Bring the idea of personal power into your everyday life. Be aware of when you are giving up your personal power and what happens when you do this. Notice when you shrink and feel small around others, and which people make you feel your power in a positive way. Be alert to when you get into comparing and what effect this has on you and your relationships.

Simply by becoming more aware, you will build your personal power. Masters from the world's spiritual traditions attest to the power of awareness itself to create change. If we do not become aware of how and when we give up our personal power, then we unconsciously do it again and again, and wonder why we feel so powerless. Simply practicing awareness with this or any of the exercises in this book will guarantee an increase in your personal and spiritual powers.

Medicine from the Natural World

Physical movement is what helps this chakra. Get your running shoes on! Or get in your wheelchair and move those arms! To help bring this chakra into balance, get outside and do some vigorous physical exercise. This could be jogging, biking, walking, hiking up a steep hill, or lying on the ground and doing some sit-ups. Spend at least thirty minutes outside doing something active. Fill your lungs up with fresh air and feel the muscles and strength of your body. Feel your physical autonomy and strength as you push your body to work and move. Try a power walk, pumping your arms and legs as you affirm to yourself: "I feel the power that is within me." Feel the power of your body. Feel the burn!

FOURTH CHAKRA: THE CHAKRA OF LOVE

The fourth chakra, known as the heart chakra, is located in the center of the chest. It is the middle chakra, connecting the three lower chakras with the three upper chakras. The heart chakra is the center of the Rainbow Body. It is considered the seat of the soul, because it is where the soul resides in the body. This chakra holds your love and compassion. It gives you the power to forgive and to release the past so you can begin again. It holds your hope and trust, along with your ability to heal others and yourself. The information and exercises in chapter 8 are aimed at enhancing the health and well-being of the heart chakra.

"Each of life's challenges is a lesson in some aspect of love."
—CAROLINE MYSS, AUTHOR OF *ANATOMY OF THE SPIRIT*

"Being a friend to yourself is no mere metaphor or purely sentimental idea. It is the basis of all relationship, because it is a fundamental recognition of the soul."
—THOMAS MOORE, FROM *SOUL MATES*

When the heart chakra is balanced, it fills you with a sense of self-acceptance and love. Opening your heart to give and receive love is one of the most important pursuits you can undertake, because to live from the heart is to be truly free.

When the heart chakra is out of balance, you may appear to be a caring and loving person but do not really feel this inside. You may have a hard time asking for what you want and accepting what others offer. You may feel resentful but not sure what is causing this feeling. You may find that you lack trust in others and often isolate yourself. If you feel numb and not really in touch with your own energy or the energy of those around you, this is an indication of an imbalance in your heart chakra.

When this chakra is blocked, it interferes with your ability to let go of the past. (You may have trouble letting go of high school and your dependent years if you are approaching graduation.) A blocked or out-of-balance heart chakra may cause you to have difficulty breathing, to feel overly jealous, to be unable to forgive yourself or others, to lack emotional connection with others, and to feel a sense of hopelessness. The most common problem found in this chakra is an absence of self-love; and if we don't love ourselves, we cannot really love anyone or anything else.

Shedding Your Old Skin

Self-acceptance is essential to our physical, spiritual, and emotional well-being. One powerful way to practice self-acceptance is to let ourselves begin again whenever we need to. Like the snake, you can shed the old skin and be green again. You can let go of the past instead of carrying it around with you. Any time you feel discouraged or feel like giving up, choose instead to give up your old "skin" and allow yourself to begin again with a new skin—a new approach.

When you do this, you let go of whatever mistakes you made and whatever wrong was done to you by other people, and allow yourself a fresh start.

Without the ability to forgive and begin again you can get really stuck. This does not mean condoning what others may have done to you. It means that you are no longer carrying the pain of what they did to you in your energy body. You might need to just let go of a difficult school year or of your identity with a particular place or group of people. It is part of the natural flow of life to begin again and again, even if it is simply starting a new semester or another day.

Is it time for you to shed a worn-out skin and begin again?

"We have it in our power to begin the world again."
—THOMAS PAINE,
REVOLUTIONARY WAR ACTIVIST

"I pretty much messed up my first two years of high school and only had my junior and senior years to save. But I felt so down and stuck. How could I change with all the same old friends and teachers after me? I decided to begin again and that if I needed to begin again a hundred times before I got through school, I would. I started meditating the summer before my junior year and this helped a lot. It was hard to give up pot because most of my friends smoked pot, but in the long run it helped with my friendships too. I am almost finished with my junior year and things are way better. I'd say I have shed a lot of old skin this year."

—RACHEL, AGE 17

The affirmations for the fourth chakra are:

I have the right to love and to be loved.
I forgive myself for all the mistakes I have made.
Today I begin again.

Snakeskin Meditation

Give yourself about ten minutes for this meditation. This can be done alone, with a friend, or in a group. Sit in a chair with your feet on the ground. Breathe and relax, . . . bring your awareness into the moment by feeling your breath in your body. Do the grounding meditation (see page 37).

Imagine in front of you an image of yourself. Breathe naturally, without effort . . . Now imagine a skin around your body that is ready to shed. Continue to breathe and imagine without effort . . . Notice what this skin may be made of. Ask the skin to give you images and thoughts of what it represents—maybe an old relationship, a negative attitude, last year, an embarrassment, a fear . . . Take a few minutes to let these images and thoughts appear. What will be shed with this old skin? . . . Now take a deep breath and imagine yourself shaking off this old skin. Just let the skin fall off . . . let the gravity of the earth help pull it down off you, falling in scraps around your feet . . . Feel all the negative memories of this skin fall away from you too . . . Now see an image of yourself, free of the old skin and standing before you, smooth and green and new . . . ready to begin again. Have this image come to you and cover you, so this new green energy body surrounds you. Breathe and sit in this new, spring green skin.

When you slowly open your eyes, take a few minutes to journal your experience. What did you shed in the old skin? What did you feel as the old skin was shed from your body and you saw yourself green and new? What does it mean for you to begin again, now?

Connecting the Fourth and Second Chakras

It is important to connect the fourth chakra and the second chakra. To make this connection, imagine a clear channel running between the two chakras. This channel connects the energy of the two chakras: pleasure seeking with compassion. This connection fosters greater safety in your relationships because your powerful senses and emotions will be guided and moderated by your love and compassion. Of course, this love and compassion must always extend to yourself. You are less likely to give yourself away to someone who doesn't care about you when your second and fourth chakras are connected. I recommend that you take the time to do this exercise while you are with a potential boy or girl friend. Then ask yourself the question: "Does this person care about me?" Ask this question from the heart center. Then listen for the internal answer, which will come from your heart chakra.

- The color of this chakra is green.
- The Bach Flower remedies for this chakra are Aloe Vera, Borage, and Bleeding Heart.
- A stone to heal and balance the fourth chakra is rose quartz. Rose quartz stimulates the energy center of the heart, helping send its energy throughout one's body. It is considered the stone of self-love. It can be used to bring love to any area of the body that has been abused or hurt. Hold it over your heart and let its properties fill your entire being with love.
- The element of the fourth chakra is air.

"To love oneself is the beginning of a lifelong romance."
—OSCAR WILDE, IRISH POET AND DRAMATIST

Medicine from the Natural World

If you can, go to a place that gives you access to a medicine wheel. A medicine wheel is a spiritual tool that allows the people using it to attune themselves to the powers of earth, the four directions, and their own spiritual source. You may want to build your own medicine wheel or medicine circle with friends. A basic medicine wheel consists of a cross within a circle, which represents the four directions (north, south, east, and west). It is referred to as a medicine wheel because it is a place where you receive earth medicine and recharge your own medicine.

"To the North American Indian, 'medicine' meant more than a substance to restore health and vitality to a sick or maladjusted body. Medicine was energy—a vital power or force that was inherent in Nature itself. A person's medicine was their power— the expression of their own life-energy system. 'Medicine Wheel' meant a circle of generated energy under the control of mind, which provided knowledge of that power. 'Medicine,' then, is personal empowerment."

—KENNETH MEADOWS, SHAMANIC PRACTITIONER AND
AUTHOR OF *EARTH MEDICINE*

Medicine Wheel Meditation

To make your own simple medicine circle, obtain some corn flour, bird or flower seeds, flower petals, or some small rocks. Find a place in a natural setting where you can sit for fifteen to thirty minutes undisturbed. With the objects you've brought, make a circle on the ground large enough for you to sit in. As you lay the objects down on the earth to make the circle, call in the energies of the earth and sky.

When the circle is completed, place yourself in the middle of it. Sit comfortably on the ground.

Notice how you are sitting on the earth, dependent on it in every way. Feel this dependence as love, the connecting force between all living things. Consider how you are connected to the animals that may be nearby. Do they not breathe the same air as you? Do they not love the warmth of the sun, like you? Think about how every living thing goes through the same cycle of birth, death, and rebirth again and again. Perhaps you have a pet that has given you great comfort in times of difficulty. Bring to your mind the love you have for this animal and the love this animal has for you. Remember a time when you felt truly loved by someone. Perhaps you were young and it was your mother. Feel the love from this memory fill you up. Feel this connection and continue to open your heart to yourself and to the world around you. Sit in this circle remembering the times of love you have experienced, and fill your heart chakra with pure love.

Now send out the love you're connecting with to every cell, every molecule, and every atom of your body . . . keep the memory and flow of love moving through you. Feel again your body on the earth and how its love sustains you and will always sustain you . . . Open your heart center to the connection that is always there. Sit in this circle of love that is connected to all and to everything.

When you are ready, you can leave the circle of flour or seeds for the earth to absorb or for the birds to eat. If you have made it out of stone, it can be left to be revisited again and again. Kenneth

Meadows' book, *Earth Medicine,* has simple directions for making a medicine wheel out of stones.

The heart chakra is also the gateway to using your psychic skills. Without a balanced heart center, shamans and healers would not succeed at their work. You cannot truly engage the powers of the upper chakras without having given some serious attention to your heart center.

"Like an ability or a muscle, hearing your inner wisdom is strengthened by doing it."

—Robbie Gass, author of *Chanting: Discovering Spirit in Sound*

"The position of the artist is humble. He is essentially a channel."

—Piet Mondrian, Dutch painter

Fifth Chakra: The Chakra of Self-Expression and Communication

The fifth chakra is located in the middle of the throat. This chakra is all about hearing your inner truth and expressing it to the world. It is the chakra of communication, sound, and creative expression. The fifth chakra is about letting your inner self and your creativity come forth. Its main function is communication, including communication with your higher self. It is about speaking your truth.

As Anodea Judith puts it, "[S]elf-expression . . . is a gateway between the inner world and the outer. Only through self-expression does the outer world get to know what's inside of us. Only through self-expression do we put forth what we have previously taken in."

The fifth chakra represents your voice and how you take your truth out into the world. At this time in your life, it is vital that you are speaking up and getting heard. If you have a balanced fifth chakra, communication comes easily for you and you speak your truth clearly and with respect for others. When the fifth chakra is out of balance you may get sore throats, have difficulty speaking up, and find it hard to hear or understand others.

This chakra is very important during your teen years. Your ability to express yourself clearly and confidently is vital to finding your true place in the world. This means finding your own voice—not necessarily the voice of your friends or parents. A person who has a blocked fifth chakra will often just say what others want to hear, rather than speak his or her own truth. Your unique individuality can only be fully expressed when you dare to express your own truth.

Without the ability to hear and speak our own truth, we end up living other people's lives, not our own.

JOSÉ'S STORY

José was eighteen and getting ready to graduate from high school. He was worried that he wouldn't succeed at his dream to be a chef and own a restaurant someday. His parents were divorced and his mother was in a controlling, emotionally abusive relationship. His father expressed sadness that he wouldn't be able to achieve his dream of living off the land in Tennessee someday. José described how his parents viewed the future: "My mother doesn't seem to really have any dreams. She is pretty stuck in her ways. I can't really speak up with her about my thoughts and dreams. She doesn't really believe in anything. My dad is open to this stuff, though. Only, he is waiting for all of his kids to grow up before he moves away and lives his dream. It is hard at times to trust my own truth when my parents are struggling so much."

I asked José how his parents' lost dreams or lack of dreaming affected him right now. "I guess it makes it hard for me to imagine what is really possible for me when my parents seem to not be able to do it. They both seem to be living a lie."

"Nothing has a stronger influence psychologically on their environment and especially on their children than the unlived life of the parent."

—CARL JUNG,
FOUNDER OF
ANALYTIC PSYCHOLOGY

Chanting a Mantra to Find Your Own Voice

Singing and chanting are ancient ways to awaken our energy body and to express ourselves. Mantras are sung for many reasons: for healing, wisdom, awareness, cleansing, balancing, and to elicit compassion. Beth Wortzel teaches groups the power of chanting and singing (see Resources). She tells of a time in the 70s when she was traveling through India on the slow train. The train would stop and fill up with local workers at the end of the day. For a short while they would ride in silence until one person would begin a chant; soon the entire car was chanting together.

Beth reminds us that chanting and singing are practices that we have lost in our modern culture, with all its noises and distractions. But chanting and singing connect us with our inner truth, with each other, and with our spiritual source. It is also a way for us to hear ourselves. Our entire body vibrates with our own voice when we chant. Chanting is also known for balancing all the chakras, and along with breathing can awaken all the positive energies in each chakra. Here's a simple chant that will massage the fifth chakra and awaken all the energies throughout the Rainbow Body.

Take a deep breath in and on the out breath make the sound OM-AH. Om is the universal sound for meditation and Ah is the sound of life, of breath. So try it: Breathe in and on the out breath chant OMMMMMM–AHHHHHH. The effect is even more potent when the chant is done in a group. You can chant with music, a simple drumbeat, or just the sound of your voice. Make sure to breathe deeply and feel the chant throughout the body. Do this for five to ten minutes. When you are finished, sit for a few moments feeling the energy of chanting.

It can be difficult for you to hear your truth when your parents have not been able to hear theirs. As you venture farther from the family home and go out on your own more, it is time for you to shed the fears and broken dreams of your parents or other adults close to you. You may want to release your parents' fears and regrets by burning them in a fire or burying them in the ground. Determine to no longer "hear" their fears and failed dreams but to hear the truth about your own future and to open up to what is possible for you now and tomorrow.

The affirmation for the fifth chakra is:

I can hear and speak my truth.

- The color of this chakra is bright blue.
- The Bach Flower remedies for this chakra are Clematis, Iris, and Blackberry.
- A stone to help heal the fifth chakra is turquoise. The healing properties of turquoise have been recognized in many ancient as well as present-day cultures. It is used for helping people to be safe and grounded when doing psychic work. It is considered a healer of one's spirit, and is used to calm and bring peace of mind to the bearer. It is highly esteemed in both Tibetan and Native American cultures.
- The element of the fifth chakra is sound.

Medicine from the Natural World

Go out to a place where you can listen to the sounds of nature. Find a spot to sit quietly and listen. Notice all the sounds that come from

"Consciousness is the ability to release the old and embrace the new with the awareness that all things end at the appropriate time and that all things begin at the appropriate time."
—CAROLINE MYSS, MEDICAL INTUITIVE

around and above you—the songs of birds, the crunching of leaves as a small animal moves nearby, the rustle of the wind, the crack of a tree limb . . . listen to the sounds that are always there but often go unnoticed.

"I went out and sat in my friend's prairie. And up in the woods I heard what I thought was drumming or maybe a motor starting up. About every three minutes the drumming sound would come again. Then I heard movement of some small creature in the grass nearby and the sounds of the prairie grass moving up against me. I felt strangely 'extended,' and the world around me was full of a lot more sound than I ever imagined. And it stirred something in me. When I returned to my friend's house I told him about the drumming and he said it was a grouse drumming the air with its feathers. They do this to announce their presence, to let the other grouse know they are there! I thought how cool it was to hear it, and how I now need to go out and announce my presence to the world!"

—MATT, AGE 17

Even if you can only get to a city park, notice the sounds of nature alive and active—open up your hearing sense to the natural world. The sounds of nature will always be able to awaken your spiritual and psychic skills. To be still enough to listen deeply will stir and awaken you, enabling you to hear what is inside and around you. I once spent ten days at a meditation retreat in "noble silence" (not talking or looking at anyone). Early one morning I was awakened by a soft humming sound. I lay still for a minute, listening . . . and discovered that I was listening to the sound of my own body's vibration.

SIXTH CHAKRA: THE PSYCHIC CHAKRA

This chakra is located at your forehead, between your eyes and just above your eyebrows, and is called the third eye. The sixth chakra is your intuitive chakra. It becomes activated during your teen years— a time when you are more able to "see" intuitively. This chakra is where your "aha's" come from—those insights that bring everything together and make sense out of your life situations. When this chakra is open, it allows you to see the big picture and to find the purpose to your life. From this chakra, you develop a personal vision of your self.

This is the chakra of insight, imagination, dreams, symbols, and images. Your sensitivity in these areas develops rapidly during your teen years. Take a moment and notice what symbols you are attracted to—spirals, arrows, Celtic crosses, flames? They all hold some personal and spiritual meaning for you. Those symbols that just seem to appear to you are symbols from spirit. For example, if you continue to doodle spirals or keep coming across spirals, you may want to look up the meaning of this symbol in a symbol dictionary (see Resources).

The development of your intuition brings forth your psychic and visionary abilities and is the main function of the sixth chakra. The purpose of the sixth chakra is to see all that is within you and around you from a place of vision and mystery. When this chakra is open and developed, you will experience your psychic nature more fully. (For more exercises to develop your psychic powers, refer to chapter 7.)

"From an energy point of view, every choice that enhances our spirits strengthens our energy field; and the stronger our energy field, the fewer our connections to negative people and experiences."

—CAROLINE MYSS,
MEDICAL INTUITIVE

Indicators of an unbalanced sixth chakra are hearing problems, earaches, headaches, and nightmares.

Doubt is the distortion of the sixth chakra. Doubt can be like the drop of ink in a clear glass of water—all the water turns the color of the ink. Doubt permeates your mind and mood and makes you hesitate when what you need is to trust yourself. Doubting yourself and your intuitive powers, and doubting the existence of spirit, can keep you from taking the necessary risks to move out freely into your independence. The more you trust yourself and your spiritual source, the more receptive you will be to flashes of wisdom and insight. What is asked of you is not to try to be completely free of doubt but rather to see what lies beyond it.

> "I really have a hard time trusting this stuff. I want to but I am afraid that in the end nothing will really work out for me. My father died when I was eight and my mother never remarried or recovered. For months after he died my mother would go around the house crying, 'Please, God, bring him back.' At eight years old I thought God would bring him back, and when my dad never did come back I felt really confused and scared. I guess I am still scared that nothing really works out and that God doesn't really listen."
>
> —AMY, AGE 16

Amy admits that God has disappointed her and that she is wary of trusting him again. Yet her inner voice seems to be saying that there is a place in her life for trusting a higher power: "Maybe I need to rethink my relationship with God. I can't seem to give up on the idea of him completely, but the relationship has got to change!" Amy is trusting herself to decide how this important relationship can work for her. In time, she will no doubt piece together a personal vision of

"To understand our place in a situation we must be able to hear and trust our inner wisdom, our intuition. No matter how beautiful and wise someone else's advice may be, always follow your own truth."

—JULIE TALLARD JOHNSON,
I CHING FOR TEENS

how God can be a source of peace and strength in her life. And that is the essence of the sixth chakra—letting in the light. It is about exploring the possibility that as yet undiscovered truths can bring you greater peace and fulfillment.

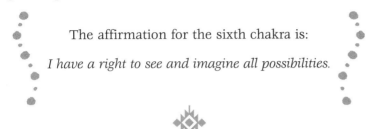

The affirmation for the sixth chakra is:

I have a right to see and imagine all possibilities.

Opening the Third Eye

Begin by grounding and breathing . . . sit in awareness of the breath for a few breaths and then bring your awareness to your sixth chakra, your third eye. Bring your attention to this chakra by imagining the in breath coming through your third eye, the spot in the center of your forehead just above your eyebrows. Now imagine that breath filling and waking up the third eye and moving down into your body. On each in breath, move the breath through the third eye and down the path of the chakras, filling up your throat chakra, then your heart chakra, moving all the way down to your first chakra. Breathe and imagine. Breathe in through your third eye and on the out breath move the energy through your body. Fill up your being with this psychic energy being filtered through your third eye . . . Then take a couple of deep breaths and rest in this energy.

Take the time to journal your experience, what you noticed in your body and what you noticed in your thoughts.

When you bring in your breath and awareness through the third eye, you are activating the energy of this chakra—imagination, psychic

"There are many ways to God."

—ARAPAHO SAYING

abilities, and vision—and awakening the other chakras with the energy of the third eye. Remember: Simply focusing breath and awareness will activate the attributes of a given chakra.

This is a particularly appropriate meditation for the teen years, when the sixth chakra is developing. One reason why you are so sensitive during your teen years is that your third eye is opening up and you are seeing more of the truth around you. This meditation will help you connect with your psychic and intuitive energy and use it to make sense of what you see.

Consulting Oracles

One way the ancients and spiritual practitioners today empower their psychic abilities is through the consulting of an oracle. Oracles are tools for contacting the spiritual powers inside and outside of you for insight and direction. An oracle is a vehicle that helps build your trust in your inner wisdom and loosen the grip of doubt. You learn to trust your intuition and the guidance of spirit more and more as you use them. Oracles are like a compass through the psychic and spiritual wilderness—a sure and reliable guide. The two most recommended oracles for building your intuition and personal power are the I Ching and the Tarot. Both oracles speak the language of the soul. They help you make choices based on ancient wisdom that has been consulted for thousands of years. These oracles work directly on building your intuition, personal power, and inner independence.

Listening to Your Dreams

Working with your dreams will help develop the sixth chakra. Dreams help you experience the world symbolically, to interpret your life in a spiritual way and to tap into the Great Mystery that is

"Tarot cards are wonderful for meditation. They act to stimulate the intuition, which is the gateway of the unconscious. They illuminate the hidden forces in our lives, of which often we are not aware. Yet these inner issues are secretly shaping the course of life. The Tarot, properly used, reveals them."

—M. J. ABADIE, *TAROT FOR TEENS*

Drawing the Chakras

A great tool to help balance and open this chakra is to draw a picture of each of your chakras. This will give you a physical record of what you see with your imagination. Get some paper and some chalk, markers, or colored pens. Give yourself at least thirty minutes for this meditation. Since you have already practiced visiting the chakras (page 63), use this same technique to focus on each chakra now, one at a time.

Get yourself in a meditative posture and check out the first chakra. Notice whether it is open or closed (trust what comes). Breathe . . . now choose the colors that you feel represent the energy of the given chakra. Draw shapes and symbols that express the energy of this chakra. Trust what comes. Color and breathe . . .

Do the same for each chakra. You can use one large sheet for all of the chakras, drawing them in the order of their positions in the body. Or you can have a separate sheet for each chakra. When you are finished, look at your drawings. What stands out for you? Do you see where you are more open or blocked? What symbols appear in certain chakras? Do the chakras appear connected to each other in some way? What do these chakra drawings tell you about yourself? Keep this in your psychic journal to refer to later. You may want to draw your chakras again, after you've done more exercises from this book.

part of us all. Dreams are another way to listen to your intuitive self and to connect with your spiritual source.

As you open up more and more psychically and energetically, your night dreams will often appear during the day, and even become part of your day life. The red-tailed hawk has always been a totem animal for me, showing up at various times and places with a message and blessing from Spirit. Two circled my wedding ceremony; one sat outside my window the day my daughter was born and again the day I brought her home from the birthing center. I've always wanted a red-tailed hawk to bless me with a feather, as this is known to be a sign of receiving a given bird's medicine. Last year I dreamt that a red-tailed hawk flew above me and dropped down one of its feathers to me. Because I believe in the power of dreams, I felt blessed by the red-tailed hawk. The next morning I went for my daily walk. As I hiked down the driveway I saw at my feet a red-tailed hawk feather. I felt twice blessed!

To open up to the wisdom and blessings of your dreams, you need to remember them. You can do this by putting out the intention at night before you sleep that you will remember your dreams, and by recording your dreams in your psychic journal. For more on dream work, see pages 188–191.

- The color of this chakra is indigo.
- The Bach Flower remedies for this chakra are Mullein, Lotus, and Cerato.
- A stone to help heal and strengthen the sixth chakra is lapis lazuli. Lapis is a combination of minerals and is dark blue in color. It holds ancient sacred properties believed to help its bearer understand sacred texts. It is used to bring awareness and clarity to spiritual issues, which makes it ideal for activating the sixth chakra.
- The element of the sixth chakra is light.

"By learning to contact, listen to and act on our intuition, we can directly connect to the higher power of the universe and allow it to become our guiding force."

—SHAKTI GAWAIN, MOTIVATIONAL AUTHOR

Medicine from the Natural World

In several of the guided meditations in this book I suggest you go to a special place in nature that you enjoy. For some it is in their backyards, a spot near a creek, a favorite tree or field. Go to that place now physically and take some time to relax and enjoy your surroundings. Take your psychic journal along with you, and some colored pens or markers. Give yourself an hour to be in this place, unrushed. Find a place to sit and let its energy and beauty and peace restore you. Write in your journal about the exercises you are doing in this book. This would also be a good place to do the Chakra Drawing or to practice the third eye meditation.

When you've been in this place for a while, take some time to notice what is new about it. What has changed since you last visited here? Is there a new plant, has something been removed or added? Is the path to the place more worn down? Notice if this change has any impact on your feelings while you are there. Be as present and involved in the place as possible. Be imaginative with this favored place by writing or drawing your experience.

Before you leave, give thanks to the earth, in your own way, for giving you such a wonderful place to visit.

"During the teen years, there may be a dawning interest in spiritual matters, mythology, or symbolism, whether through music, lyrics, popular movie icons, or the latest fashion at school."

—ANODEA JUDITH, FROM *EASTERN BODY, WESTERN MIND*

SEVENTH CHAKRA: THE CHAKRA OF DIVINE WISDOM

The seventh chakra, also called the crown chakra, is located at the top of your head. Caroline Myss, an authority on psychic development, refers to this chakra as our Spiritual Connector. She writes, "The seventh chakra is our connection to our spiritual nature and our capacity to allow our spirituality to become an integral part of our physical lives and guide us." This chakra allows us to connect with the divine—our spiritual source—in a personal and meaningful way. The divine is another expression for the Tao, or the Great Mystery, God, Goddess, or the Creator. It is the limitless source of spiritual energy that moves through everything and everyone.

When this chakra is open, you can understand the greatest mysteries of life. To completely open the crown chakra takes years and years of learning meditations and other spiritual practices, and studying with a spiritual adviser such as a guru, meditation teacher, transpersonal psychotherapist, shamanic practitioner, or Zen master. At the end of chapter 9 you can find out how to contact such teachers.

Note: Energy practitioners recommend that you activate the seventh chakra only after you have opened up the other six chakras.

Presently, in your teen years, the energy of the seventh chakra pulls you toward seeking this connection with the divine and its wisdom. So, to begin the process of opening your crown chakra, be attentive to this internal tug to connect with spirit. The best techniques for opening the seventh chakra are those that teach us how to be present in the moment. Opening up to the Great Mystery, the Divine, is not something that is going to happen tomorrow—it happens now, in this moment, in this very place. The divine is always available to you. Practices such as mindfulness meditations, monitoring your thoughts, and consciously focusing your full attention on whatever activity you are engaged in all make it possible for you to experience the presence of the divine in everything you do. The exercises throughout this book can help bring you more and more into the moment and into a very real connection with your spiritual source and your true nature.

"Stop thinking and talking about it and there is nothing you will not be able to know."
—ZEN PARADIGM

"I can't really describe what I felt when we meditated as a group. It was really incredible—I felt some connection to everything. It was both peaceful and intense. I didn't realize I could have such a feeling so quickly and so naturally."

—JOEL, AGE 18

Going into psychic trance and engaging in shamanic journeying both engage the seventh chakra. Chapter 7 offers exercises and meditations for journeying and for going into trance, as well as for connecting with your spiritual source.

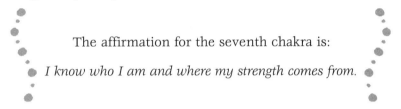

The affirmation for the seventh chakra is:

I know who I am and where my strength comes from.

Prayers

Prayer is a time-honored technique for engaging the seventh chakra. Virtually all spiritual practices include forms of prayer. There are countless ways to pray, to send out a request to your spiritual source for help and guidance. After practicing different techniques you will choose what kind of prayer works for you. My morning prayers include asking my source for guidance in all that I think, do, and say that day. I believe that calling on our spiritual source for this help brings this help to us.

Sometimes the idea of prayer, or asking for help from a higher power, seems futile. This is often because of some past experience we have had with religion. Many teenagers share with me that they had a religion forced on them and now want to be left alone. Yet they feel very alone at times without any sense of a spiritual connection. The power of the seventh chakra is gained through practices

"We always have a choice: we can limit our perception so that we close off vastness, or we can allow vastness to touch us."

—CHÖGYAM TRUNGPA,
SHAMBHALA: THE SACRED PATH OF THE WARRIOR

that invite such a spiritual connection. This connection is always to a spiritual source that is positive, compassionate, and bigger than any problems in your life. If you feel completely disconnected from any such source, chances are this chakra is blocked or not yet developed. You may want to pray to have your higher power reveal itself to you.

The following chapters offer many ways to receive guidance from spirit.

- The color of this chakra is violet.
- The Bach Flower remedies for this chakra are Star Tulip and Lotus.
- A stone to help heal the seventh chakra is clear quartz. Quartz is considered a mineral that transforms energy. This stone is believed to be able to assist you in calling the power of spirit into your soul and is used to help communicate with the spirit world. It is used to activate the crown chakra.
- Smoky quartz is helpful in grounding all the energy in the body from the crown chakra to the first (root) chakra. Amber helps clean out all the chakras. You may visualize the energies of these stones or hold a stone in your hand and imagine its energy moving throughout your entire body and filling up each chakra.

Medicine from the Natural World

Find a tree that you can sit up against for about ten minutes without being disturbed. Find a place at the base of the tree where you can rest your back comfortably against the trunk. Take a moment to ground.

Relax in the breath and imagine yourself as part of this tree, with your roots going down deep into the ground, getting nourishment from mother earth . . . Feel your branches reaching up and out to the sky, pulling in the energy of the sun and the blue sky . . . Make sure that branches are reaching up out of your crown chakra. Breathe . . . You and the tree are one—dependent on the earth and the heavens for your nourishment. Your crown chakra is open to the sun's rays, which pour down into your entire being. Sit for a few minutes, taking in all this nourishment. Notice how true it is that you and the tree are one and that you do know who you are and where your strength comes from.

Addictions and the Chakras

It is easy to become addicted in our culture. In fact, you may often feel encouraged and supported to be addicted to something or someone. At first, all addictions are an attempt to feel good and to reach some altered state of consciousness. Sometimes they are used to deal with stress, like using alcohol to calm your anxiety, video games to avoid commitments, or fanatical religious beliefs to allay your fears. But the benefits of the given substance or practice soon turn into a hazard and begin to harm you, throwing your life out of balance.

Behaviors and practices qualify as addictions when they follow a habitual pattern and you give up your personal power to the substance

"If you feel the real joy and the real spirit within you, they come out naturally. If you really go deep inside, everything is there. You feel it and, if you want it to come out, it will come out."

—Mayumi Oda,
Japanese-American
Artist and Activist

The Chakras and Related Addictions

Chakra seven:	fanatical religious beliefs and assumptions, obsessive spiritual practices
Chakra six:	hallucinogens, marijuana
Chakra five:	opiates, marijuana, video games, television
Chakra four:	tobacco, sugar, relationships, marijuana
Chakra three:	cocaine, crack, caffeine, approval/perfectionism, anger
Chakra two:	alcohol, sex, heroin, acting out, television
Chakra one:	food, shopping, gambling, perfectionism

or practice. The addiction then is more powerful than you, and your life is in trouble.

Every addiction is related to one of the chakras. Addictive behavior will keep you stuck in the negative characteristics of the associated chakra. So if you are addicted to marijuana and hallucinogens, for example, you may be stuck in doubt, fear, and distrust.

Take the time now, before reading further, to consider whether a particular behavior could be developing into an addiction for you. Working on the related chakra will certainly help, but if a behavior has already become an addiction, seeking other help will be necessary. Consider contacting a local support group, confide in a trusted adult, or seek the guidance of a nurse or therapist.

When you can live from your energy body, listen to its wisdom and messages, and tend to your energy system (the chakras), you become more and more attuned to the purpose of your life. Such living connects you to everything true and beautiful inside of you and outside of you. There really is no greater power than to feel and live this connection to truth and beauty. Certainly you have heard it said that wealth and success alone do not bring happiness. The greatest happiness does come from discovering—and living—your true potential. Every chakra can be understood as a reminder of the very real power you hold inside of you for making that life a reality.

"The I Ching teaches principles through which it may be possible to learn to live in harmony with the Tao, the invisible meaning-giving matrix of the universe."
—JEAN SHINODA BOLEN, PSYCHIATRIST, AUTHOR OF *THE GODDESS WITHIN*

"There was this young man enjoying himself fishing in this
boat out in the middle of a beautiful lake. It was one of his
favorite places to relax and hang out without
others bothering him. As he was sitting there enjoying himself,
another boat was coming toward him, fast. He shouted,
"Watch out, watch out!" But the boat
continued to move swiftly toward him. He screamed and
waved his arms about to stop the boat from hitting him,
but the boat just came faster and faster, right toward
him. He was standing and screaming at the top of his
lungs when the boat crashed right into him.
As he sailed through the air, he noticed that
the other boat didn't have anyone in it."

—ZEN STORY

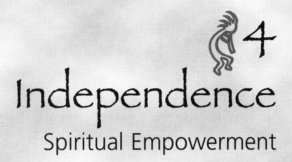

Independence
Spiritual Empowerment

4

◎ RITA'S STORY OF INDEPENDENCE ◎

I was in this relationship for almost two years where my boyfriend controlled my every move and thought. My mother, the school guidance counselor, and teachers all tried to help me but I wouldn't listen. I tried going to a therapist once and my boyfriend came with me. She saw right through him, though—and this made him even madder. He threatened that if I went to her without him he wouldn't ever talk to me again.

As the year went on I was getting thinner and having more and more difficulty in school. Anytime I would think of creating any space between us he would show up by my side. He even came to my house some nights and got me out of bed. He was controlling my every move. It is hard to explain to others how someone can begin to even control your thoughts. But he did. At the time I felt I would die without him. I was losing all my friends and my mother was desperate.

Finally, my guidance counselor and some friends got me alone and confronted me. They kept telling me how different I was, how pale and lifeless I looked. Every time I would defend myself or my boyfriend they would give me examples of how I was not even thinking right. They told me that, to them, I looked like I was dying. And I think I was dying inside. The weird thing is my older sister married someone who controlled and abused her. She has been in and out of women's shelters for years and I knew I didn't want that kind of life for myself, but here I was in a very sick relationship. I was scared of my boyfriend and I also didn't want to alienate him. My body felt little and weak.

I finally admitted that my friends were right. I ended up throwing up before I called the social services with the help of my guidance counselor and filed a restraining order on my boyfriend. I won't say that the whole story is pretty or even over. But I am determined to get my life back, to finish school, and to try and stay out of that relationship, and any other one like it.

That day, when I left the school to go home, my mother came by and picked me up. I still felt little but something inside of me was also waking up. Something that is hard to describe but something that was in me all along. It had been raining, and as we drove home together the sun came out and there was a double rainbow over the road. Somehow I felt God was sending me a message that I was doing the right thing . . . that somehow everything was going to be okay.

—RITA, AGE 16

> "Your soul has a place it wants you to travel. Listening then to the soul's message is of great importance."
> —MYRON ESHOWSKY, SHAMANIC HEALER

🌀 EAGLE BOY, BY DENNIS L. OLSON 🌀

A Zuni Pueblo boy found an eagle nestling that had fallen from its cliff home. He took the bird home and spent most of his time hunting for this bird and caring for it. His parents and relatives became very upset that the boy spent little time helping in the fields, and they decided to kill the eagle. Eagle knew what was about to happen (he could see all the way out to the fields) and told the boy he was sad that things had worked out *like this. He told the boy he must leave, for everyone's good. The boy was distraught, and begged the eagle to take him along. After much discussion, Eagle finally agreed, but the boy had to agree to pack much food and tie bells to the feet of Eagle. They left at dawn.*

Eagle Boy climbed on the back of Eagle and they rose high into the sky. The bells were jingling and they sang a lifelong song. The relatives down below cried and begged the boy to come home, but he didn't hear them. Eagle and Eagle Boy flew through a hole in the clouds and landed on the Sacred Mountain of the Eagle People. These People adopted the boy and made him a flying coat of feathers. He soon learned to fly as they did.

The Eagle People told Eagle Boy that he should never fly to the Land of Bones in the south, but his curiosity was too great for his judgment. He flew over the Land of Bones at night and saw beautiful people dancing around beautiful fires in a beautiful city. He flew down to join them and danced until he was exhausted. He fell asleep. When he woke in the morning, all he saw were dusty crumbling buildings and piles of bones. He looked for his coat of feathers, so he could fly away, but it was gone. Suddenly, the bones stood up and formed skeletons. They chased him into the den of a badger, who told the boy of a way he could climb back to the Eagle People. It took a long time, but he finally arrived at the Sacred Mountain again. The Eagle People told him he was no longer welcome there, and turned away from him. His Eagle friend took pity on him and gave him a tattered feather coat, so he could fly home to the Pueblos. He just made it—the coat disintegrated as soon as he landed. He never went back, but remembers the place above the clouds every time he sees the eagles high overhead.

THE ROAD TO INNER INDEPENDENCE

In the preceding stories we see examples of young people seeking independence—finding their own way apart from the expectations and demands of others. But true independence is really experienced from within. It is not dependent on how others see you or whether others approve of you or not. It comes from really being true to yourself and believing in yourself. To find your place as an adult in the world and to fulfill your purpose, you must first acquire some inner independence. And that means you must be willing to venture outward (and inward) to "risky places."

Each of us must be willing to go to our own "risky places" to become who we truly are. Sometimes this will mean actually travelling to a new, unfamiliar place, as Eagle Boy did. Other times it will mean taking an emotional risk, as Rita did when she chose to be alone rather than stay in an abusive relationship. Like Eagle Boy and Rita, you are poised to take your first step out into the world that calls to you. On this trip, you will discover your limits while you gain insights about who you really are.

Eagle Boy needed to follow the flight of the eagle. But he ignored the eagle's advice about the bone people, and he learned from this mistake. He had to return home again, but only after going on a great journey. Certainly this first pilgrimage out helped prepare him for his continued journey of independence. Who knows what will call him next to move beyond his childhood into his adult life? What is calling you right now? What advice have you been given? What advice are you ignoring, like Eagle Boy?

Soon you will embark on your own flight, with its perils, lessons, and rewards. With every decision and every misstep, you will learn more about yourself and the world around you.

"My parents didn't want me to go out west after graduation. But I knew I had to go. A group of us were heading to the Grand Canyon to sleep out under the stars. I got sick on the road, and a lot of the

"To awaken a spiritual authority, an inner sense of knowing, always involves a shift of identity, a rebirth, a recovery of spirit. In the Buddhist tradition we speak of this as finding our True Nature."

—JACK KORNFIELD, BUDDHIST MONK, AUTHOR OF *A PATH WITH HEART*

others were fighting with each other. The one girl I connected with left early. I had little money, and took only bagels and peanut butter with me into the canyon. But the canyon was awesome. I cannot put it into words what effect the whole trip had on me, even the difficulties. All I can say is I left a kid and I am no longer a kid.

"I feel the hugeness of it all—leaving for college this fall, having to find my own meals every day, making decisions for myself now. I am back with my parents for the summer but will leave again to attend the School Without Boundaries in Colorado, where I will be out in the desert by myself for four nights. I will make more mistakes but I know I will come back even stronger and wiser. I was afraid to go off to school, and actually I am still some, but I realize now it is what I must do—move out and move on."

—ALI, AGE 18

Like Eagle Boy, you may have to travel to risky places, both internal and external, to claim your independence and discover your place in the world.

Consider your risky places with this in mind: If it doesn't cause any harm to yourself or others, it may be a risk you need to take. There are no guarantees, of course. You might try to convince yourself that you are not harming yourself or others, when in fact you would be. You might get hurt. You might not. The intuitive skills and confidence you will gain from this book will help you to know which risks are worth taking.

I know this young man who is not going to these risky places. His name is Joel. Joel is a creative, loving young man of eighteen who is a friend to many. He is also an addict. His drug addiction is not a risky place—it's actually a comfortable place for him. It keeps him home with his father, who also abuses drugs. It stops him from moving out, trying new places. He dreams of going off to school but he hasn't

"It is not because things are difficult that we do not dare; it is because we do not dare that they are difficult."
—SENECA, ROMAN PHILOSOPHER AND STATESMAN

"Not knowing when the dawn will come, I open every door."
—EMILY DICKINSON, AMERICAN POET

"Sometimes I go about pitying myself, But all the while I am being carried by great winds across the sky . . ."
—OJIBWE SONG

moved. He needs to risk getting free of his addiction. He needs to risk being independent. All sorts of feelings and fears will pop up once he is straight and on his own. That is the risky place he needs to go.

When fears surface for you, it can often mean there a risky place beckoning you to visit. What fears are coming up for you these days? What steps do you need to take to bring yourself closer to those internal and external risky places that are worth investigating? Remember, fear is not necessarily a sign that you shouldn't do something—it's simply an indication that you are considering doing something that involves some kind of risk for you.

When you decide that it is important for you to take a risk, you will find that you are on your own, but you are not alone. Rita, in the earlier story, was afraid that when she left her boyfriend she would be alone, but instead she felt herself connected to something much greater. It's a paradox: Your individuality—your inner independence—is what enables you to really feel the connection to all things. A wheel is made up of many individual parts; with one missing part it doesn't work so well. Each part of our body is dependent on the others but each also has its unique and independent purpose. So it is with you. You are a vital part of the entire wheel of life, which includes everything and everyone. When you are not living your dream, not expressing your uniqueness, something is out of sync for us all.

The wisdom keepers of Zen, Tibetan Buddhism, Hinduism, and mystical Christianity, to name a few, know that to encourage your individuality benefits the whole of humanity. They also know that to express your true nature is your most important goal on earth. That is why these traditions all use meditations that help bring forth your unique individuality, your true self.

"We have to accept personal responsibility for uplifting our lives."

—CHÖGYAM TRUNGPA, TIBETAN LAMA, AUTHOR OF *SHAMBHALA: THE SACRED PATH OF THE WARRIOR*

LOTUS MEDITATION

This meditation is borrowed from the yogic tradition. It helps slow the mind, calm your entire being, promote a sense of serenity, and bring you into the present moment. It will open you up to the truth about you, and help you believe in yourself and your choices.

Find a quiet place where you can meditate for at least five minutes. Sit in a meditative posture with your eyes closed. Let your breath be relaxed, let it breathe by itself . . . Bring your awareness down to your first and second chakras. Imagine that your lower body is a rich, dark soil. Breathe and imagine . . . then picture a beautiful white lotus flower growing out of this rich soil, growing up through your upper body, and coming to bloom in your heart chakra. Breathe and feel the beauty and the energy of this most sacred flower. As you imagine this, repeat to yourself several times:
"I am ready to bring forth my true nature into the world."

Feel your readiness to bring forth what is within you. Feel the truth of who you are. After you have sat with this truth for a few minutes, you can consult the lotus for guidance. Breathe into the lotus and look into its center. Look into the blossom of the lotus: Held deep within it is a helpful message for you. What truth does the lotus hold for you today? Simply breathe and ask, and then notice what comes. Trust what comes, whether it be a sentence, a word, an idea, or a symbol. Open yourself up to the truth that grows within you. Then, journal about your experience and the message you received from the lotus.

"Think of yourself as an incandescent power, illuminated and perhaps forever talked to by God and his messengers."

—BRENDA UELAND, AMERICAN WRITER, AUTHOR OF *IF YOU WANT TO WRITE*

The Lotus Flower

The lotus flower—which has its roots in the mud, but arises from it beautiful and clean—is a symbol of how we all can rise, magnificent, from the muddiest of conditions. It holds spiritual significance in many traditions. The guru who brought Buddhism to Tibet was known as Padmasambhava, "born from out of the lotus." The lotus is a symbol of creation: Out of the mud the world is born. It is also a symbol of wisdom—it expresses the truth about the possibility for all living things. The popular Buddhist mantra "Om mani Padme hum" translates as "Om, jewel in the lotus, amen." Simply reciting this mantra is known for bringing peace to the chanter and to those nearby.

BE CURIOUS ABOUT EVERYTHING

Knowing more about the world around you can help you to feel confident about your choices. So, *be curious about everything!* To be curious really means to be open minded, says Shunryu Suzuki, the great Zen master, in his book *Zen Mind, Beginner's Mind*. To be curious is to approach life with a beginner's mind—try not to assume. Instead, be curious and present for what life is offering you in this moment. A beginner's mind is open to the myriad of possibilities that the present and the future hold. When you assume too much, you shut off your curiosity and often miss an opportunity.

"My parents had arranged for me to return to this acting camp. It was fine when I was a kid, but I am seventeen now! I didn't even think much about it, I just assumed that I would have a raging

awful time. And I did have a horrible time. I sat by myself, bored, all day. I went to my bunk early every night. I didn't try anything I didn't have to. The entire weekend was trashed. The really strange thing is, my eighteen-year-old cousin, who I really respect, had a great time. I overheard her saying how awesome it was for her. Then I realized the whole trip was in my head! I hate to admit it, but I went in with a bad attitude and that made for a rotten weekend."

—JESSICA, AGE 17

Hopefully, your curiosity has been nourished and encouraged, because it is this very curiosity, or lack of it, that will help determine your life's path. Curiosity is a wonderful, powerful tool, another one of those tools that you have inside of you. Instead of just believing what you are taught, even in this book, wonder about it—bring your curiosity to it. Bring *yourself* to it. Does it feel true for you? Does it feel correct for you? There is so much to discover around you, every day, if you look beyond the face value of things and seek a deeper truth. Curiosity will enrich your life and unearth treasures that lie hidden in the most mundane places. Discovering these treasures for yourself is a powerful way to build your inner independence.

Curiosity is a great way to combat fear. When you find yourself afraid, see if you can become curious instead. Where is the fear coming from? Where is the fear in your body? What situations have had this effect on you in the past? What is really going on around you, right now, in this moment?

Breathing can help you awaken the energy and curious spirit that are inside of you. Breath is a simple yet powerful tool to free what is stuck in you and loosen up the fear and resistance that may be keeping you back. Fear makes us hold our breath—and therefore weakens us. Breathing moves the negative energy out and allows for the positive energy to emerge.

The breath exercise that follows is a good one for supporting your move toward independence. It is called Mother's Breath because when you do it, love and positive feelings from spirit enter you on the waves of your breathing.

Sufi Mother's Breath

Find a place where you can relax, and give yourself five to ten minutes to do this exercise. Sit comfortably in a chair or on the floor. Take a deep breath in and sigh (ahhhhh) on the exhale. Now breathe slowly through your nose to the count of five. Hold your breath for a moment, then exhale, again with a sigh. Empty all the breath out on the exhale. Breathe in through the nose to the count of five, hold the breath for a moment, and exhale with a sigh. Repeat several times.

Now sit, relaxed in this energy, for a few moments. Notice all the sensations in your body. Notice the thoughts that come. Take a few moments to journal if you like.

LETTING GO

Soon—maybe this month, or next year—it will be time for you to let go of high school, of some friends, of your parents. That, of course, is one of the reasons you need to develop your inner independence. At this time in your life, it's important that your parents and others who care about you let you go your own way. It is not healthy for your parents to try and mold you in their image by insisting you go to a certain college or enter their trade. Parents who try to protect their teenagers by trying to dictate everything they do will make their children weak, which actually puts them in more danger. Your parents can help you grow strong and ready for independence by letting you go in safe ways—encouraging you to take worthwhile risks to discover who you are and supporting you emotionally, financially, and spiritually to go after your dreams. You and your parents need only to copy nature—all parents in the wild push their young toward independence, and the young venture out. If they didn't, life would very quickly get out of balance.

Mother bears invest a lot of time and skill to train their cubs. When a bear cub has learned to hunt and fend for itself, its mother takes the cub out past their familiar territory. She then may sit at the bottom of some large tree while the bear cub climbs up its trunk. When the bear cub is up high enough, mother bear leaves and gets out of sight and out of the scent range of the cub.

Because the cub is having such a fine time, he doesn't notice Mom is gone for quite some time. When he does realize that he is alone, he begins to cry out for the mother bear to return. He wants to go home. He is getting hungry, and maybe a little scared. But cry as he might, mother bear does not return. Soon, the cub begins to act according to his instinct and training. He sets out to find something to eat and a place to sleep. Tomorrow he will head off to find a new territory to call his own.

What would happen if the mother bear turned around when the cub cried out and took him back home? Or what if the mother bear never guided the cub out far enough? It is natural for parents as well as teenagers to feel frightened at times as independence looms before them. It is natural for teenagers to sometimes want to go back home and stay. But first, spend some time in that new, unfamiliar place where life is pushing you—see what is there to be discovered. It's okay to be a little afraid, but give yourself time to let that fear turn into curiosity. It's time to go find and explore your own territory . . . and your own destiny.

Letting Go Meditation

Give yourself about fifteen to twenty minutes for this meditation.

Find a comfortable position. Close your eyes and take a minute to ground. Now bring your attention to your breath. Simply notice the air moving in and out of your nostrils, brushing up against the top of your nostrils as it passes. Give your body permission to relax. Bring your attention to your legs and let them relax . . . ask your genital area to relax, and your buttocks . . . breathe and relax, letting go of tension or tightness that may be there . . . relax your stomach and lower back . . . ask your chest and upper back to release any tension they may hold . . . relax and breathe . . . letting go of tension . . . letting go . . . Now move your awareness to your neck and throat, letting go of any tension there, and your shoulders and arms, relaxing and letting go . . . letting go . . . relaxing your facial muscles and letting go of any tension you may hold in your face . . . letting go of the tension that may be in the scalp and just letting go . . . letting go and relaxing.

Now imagine yourself in your bedroom at home, and you are packing your boxes and suitcases to leave. Notice what you are choosing to take and what you are leaving behind. Continue to breathe . . . Now notice that there is a box labeled THROWAWAYS. In this box you will throw away any negative beliefs, people, memories, worries, fears, attitudes, and ideas that you are holding on to in your body. Say to yourself, "I would be ready to leave if it were not for . . ." and allow for the image, person, experience, or word to emerge. When the image or person appears, place it in the box. Trust what comes . . . and breathe and relax. Continue to breathe and relax, now letting go of anything or anyone that would hold you back. Continue to say to yourself "I would be ready to leave if it were not for . . ." until no more images or ideas come to mind. When you are done filling the box, close the top and invite a "Spiritual Mover" to come and dispose of it in a safe and respectful way. Imagine a spirit helper coming in and taking away the box.

Bring your attention to your body and notice how you are feeling as your spirit helper takes away the THROWAWAY *box. Do you feel lighter? Stronger? More ready to take those risks, to begin to create your new life away from home? Take a few moments to enjoy the feelings and when you are ready bring your attention back to your breath as it moves in and out of your nostrils. Bring your awareness back to the room you are in and slowly open your eyes. Take a few moments to adjust to the room, now feeling awake and relaxed . . . and freer.*

UNCORDING: ENERGETIC INDEPENDENCE

When there seems to be something that is preventing you from feeling your independence—some powerful but invisible influence holding you back—you may have come upon an energetic cord. Cords are energetic connections we have with others. Cords can be positive as well as negative. They are often unspoken and unquestioned agreements that we will behave a certain way or fulfill a given role for another person. Some of these agreements make you unduly responsible for that other person's feelings, or imply that you behave in ways that are detrimental to your well-being. These agreements are often based on false or outdated beliefs about who you are. Such cords are unhealthy and use up your vital energy. To be strong in your freedom, you may need to break some of these cords.

"Your decision to evolve consciously through responsible choice contributes not only to your own evolution, but also to the evolution of all of those aspects of humanity in which you participate. It is not just you that is evolving through your decisions, but the entirety of humanity."

—GARY ZUKAV, AUTHOR OF *THE SEAT OF THE SOUL*

"I don't want to go right from high school into college. Mostly it is because I want to experience what it is like not to be in school. And I need to work and earn some money. My biggest fear is that I will never make it into college because I will get too caught up in working and just hanging out. I am moving to California to live with a cousin and work for a year. Everyone's telling me that if I do that, I won't end up going to college.

"But in a session with Julie I learned to 'uncord' from these unsupportive people. I realized that I was taking on all this stuff about me, that was not helping me. My boyfriend was the worst. He didn't want me to leave. I felt as if I was responsible for him, that my leaving would really hurt him. He has been out of high school for four years now and works at a local mechanic shop. He used to get high all the time and he says I am the only one that keeps him clean.

"'Uncording' from him helped me separate my feelings from his. It helped me feel my autonomy. I am just starting out my life. I feel freer to do what it is I have to do—and that is to get on with my life!"

—JOSELYN, AGE 18

Uncording is the process of energetically letting go of negative or outdated connections and agreements you have with other people. Any negative belief you hold about yourself is a sure sign that you are corded to someone. Do you hold any negative beliefs about yourself?

"I'm going to fail somehow."

"I will end up alone."

"I can't give up drugs."

"I am too afraid to try anything new."

"I always have to do better."

"I can't say no."

Cords are energetic connections to another person, based on something you are agreeing to in that relationship. So if the agreement is that you are a loser, you believe that you are a loser; you are in agreement with this belief. And this belief does not come from or reflect your true nature—it was somehow passed on to you by another person, and then you "agreed" to it and are now corded to that person through this agreement. Such negative agreements can sound like this:

"Approach this work of uncording with respect. Know that it is real and that you are altering energy. "
—COLLEEN BRENZY, INTUITIVE HEALER, PHILOSOPHER

"I won't speak up around you."

"I am a sex object."

"I will make myself smaller so you can feel bigger."

"I agree to be a failure."

"I will always be an addict."

Uncording from negative connections will free up energy for you to use in ways that are creative and meaningful for you. Remember, your body is an emotional, feeling, energetic machine, and cords impact this feeling body of yours. A "pain in the neck" may be a cord to your sister who is constantly picking on you. The agreement may be for you to be a constant bother to your sister, to provide a safe way for her to vent anger that actually is about something deeper and more threatening. Or the anxiety you experience may be about a cord you have to your mother, who fears for your future. Perhaps she had a really bad experience leaving home and now she is afraid for you. You have come into agreement with this fear and now feel anxious a lot of the time.

> *"I am afraid to leave home because my brother will be left alone on the farm. He hasn't a chance without me there. My dad will take complete control of him and he will be stuck there. He is so cool, but he is afraid of our dad. What will happen to him if I go?"*
>
> —HENRY, AGE 18

"Start a huge, foolish project, like Noah. It makes absolutely no difference, what people think of you."

—RUMI, SUFI MASTER AND POET

What might Henry's agreement be, and with whom? He probably has one with his father about staying on the farm. And with his brother, to protect him from their father. Cords are almost always tied with strong emotions. Recognizing and unraveling unhealthy cords can be a difficult and unsettling process. But ultimately, you and the person you are corded to will be stronger as a result.

> *"I am twenty-seven years old and I know I have agreed not to do better than my dad. And he works at a job he hates, smokes weed every night, and complains about my mom! I won't get out of this town and dead-end job if I don't end that agreement."*
>
> —TYLER, AGE 27

Who Are You Corded To?

The first and most important step in uncording from the negative energy of others is to become aware of the cord and its agreement. You must first name the agreement to be able to uncord from it. Sometimes you will find a cord because you have some health problem related to a given chakra (see chapter 3). Let's say you have stomachaches—you will want to check for cords related to your second and third chakras. If you have throat problems, you will want to look for cords in your throat chakra. Can you identify some family agreements that lock you into unhealthy beliefs or behavior? Can you locate the chakra that they are in?

Uncording Exercise

Allow yourself some personal, unhurried time. Sit comfortably in a chair with your feet on the floor. Have your journal nearby. Take a few minutes to ground and relax in your breath . . . feel your breath as it moves through your body. Now bring your awareness to your heart center (chakra). Inside your heart chakra is your inner healer. Ask for help from your inner healer. Ask him or her to show you where the cord is in your body. Is it in your neck, your lower back, your second chakra, your belly? Trust the answer that comes and focus your awareness on that place in your body. Ask your inner healer to also go to that place in your body. Continue to breathe and trust . . . Remain aware of your body . . . stay present in the body . . . Then ask the healer, Who is the cord connecting me to? (You may already have an idea, but new information can come now from the inner healer.) Simply ask, and trust that there will be an image or a sense of who it is. Then ask the healer to show you the agreement that is held with this cord. Continue to breathe and listen . . . Then imagine the healer asking you, "Are you ready to release this cord, and to end this agreement?" Say to the healer and to yourself, "Yes, I am ready to end this agreement and uncord from this person."

Continue to breathe and remain aware of your body. You may even notice some pain in that area of the body, which will now be released as you release the cord.

"No one can make you feel inferior without your consent."

—ELEANOR ROOSEVELT, FORMER FIRST LADY, DIPLOMAT, AND HUMANITARIAN

"We agreed to this life. No one else can can do this stuff for us, so we might as well. Time with action heals all wounds. Time alone does not heal."

—COLLEEN BRENZY, PSYCHIC HEALER, PHILOSOPHER

Visualize the cord. Imagine a hand going into the affected chakra and gently removing the cord. Now imagine a rose near the cord, and place all the negative energy from the cord into the rose. Breathe and take your time. Now blow up the rose. Gather up the scattered energy and neutralize it. Neutralize it by simply postulating that the energy is neutral. Simply sending out a thought to the energy, a new intention, the negative energy is now neutralized and can be reused. This is how we "recycle" energy. Now imagine bringing this neutral energy back down through the top of your head (the crown chakra). Breathe, and allow this energy to go to wherever in your body it wants. Then fill up the area where the cord was with your own energy. Imagine your hands and the inner healer's hands smoothing over the area that you uncorded. Make sure it is completely filled with your energy.

Thank the inner healer and see him or her returning to your heart center. Bring your attention back to the area of your body that held the cord. Notice how it feels now. Rest for a few moments in this new energy. Open your eyes slowly and reflect on your experience and what you learned about yourself. Write in your journal about the cord you have released and the agreement you have ended. Write next to your journal entry, or say out loud: "So it is. Thank you. Thank you. Thank you." This affirms the new truth you discovered and acknowledges the help you had from your inner healer and higher power.

To Uncord, Remember to Check Who, What, and Where

Who are you corded with?
What is the agreement?
Where in the body is the cord?
Do you want to *remain corded* to this person, in this way?

"I had this horrible feeling in my neck. It felt like pieces of metal. My healer went there and we found a cord to my sister. I thought I was corded to my mother but it was my older sister I was agreeing 'to act stupid' for. Somehow my acting stupid around her friends made her feel important. And she was always making fun of me. My sister always has her friends hanging around and I find I have to leave the house because I can't stand how I feel around them.

"Ending this agreement could change my life. It's neat how I have it in me to do this. Now, I know that it's not about me acting stupid. I can act however I want. So it is! Thank you. Thank you. Thank you."

—JOURNAL ENTRY FROM HEATHER, AGE 15

"One of the most coura-
geous things you can do
is identify yourself, know
who you are, what you
believe in, and where
you want to go."
—SHEILA MURRAY BETHEL,
AUTHOR OF
MAKING A DIFFERENCE

When you remove cords, you are literally altering your energy and connection to others. You may still be connected to a given person, but in a better way. Removing cords will result in changes in both your physical body and your psychological makeup. You will no longer be living according to someone else's fears or negativity. You will experience a surge in your inner independence. Others will likely feel the change too. If you are no longer agreeing to "act stupid," your changed behavior will affect that relationship.

If you are feeling stuck in your efforts to uncord a relationship, you may want to go to a craniosacral therapist, a trained energy healer, or a shamanic practitioner to help you with the uncording. He or she will work with you energetically in removing the cord from your energy body. As a result, you will notice a physical freedom where there is now physical pain. Craniosacral therapists and some other professional healers will place their hands gently on your body as they work. Most shamanic practitioners and other psychic healers will work with the energy around and outside your body. Whichever approach you prefer to assist with your uncording, a healer can really help move things along. See the resources section for finding practitioners.

Trusting Yourself

"The world is ruled by letting things take their course."

—Lao-tzu,
Chinese philosopher

"No one can give you wiser advice than yourself."

—Cicero,
Roman orator

To feel prepared and confident enough to move out on your own, it really comes down to trusting yourself. You already have a great deal of experience at this. When you entered middle school and the teen years, you were already relying on yourself for major decisions. Your parents didn't follow you to school. They weren't there when you decided to join a certain group or club. They weren't with you when you felt put down and depressed because you weren't fitting in. They haven't chosen your friends. You were on your own when your boyfriend or girlfriend wanted to have sex, or when your best friend offered you a joint.

Still, at this point in your life you may find the choices and changes that lie ahead overwhelming. So how is it that some people get confident and sure of themselves and their choices? How do you come to fully trust yourself?

Mindfulness Meditation

One of the surest ways to build trust in yourself and embrace independence is to have a regular meditation practice. Meditation stills the discursive thought patterns in your head long enough so you can hear the call of your heart and awaken to your true nature. When your mind is still enough, you can hear that inner truth and act upon it. Meditation encourages you to simply be with things as they are—not calling them good or bad, letting whatever thoughts and emotions arise dissolve, not holding on to anything. Being able to still the mind in this way empowers you beyond measure because you learn how to be present for whatever comes up in your life. This is true independence!

Give yourself ten minutes for this meditation. It can be read out loud or taped and played back to you for the first several times.

Get yourself in a meditative posture with your back in an upright, alert position, not resting against anything. You can be sitting in a chair with your feet on the floor, or on a meditation cushion. Just sit for a few breaths, in this body, bringing your awareness to the breathing, sitting body . . . Now just rest in the breath . . . noticing the physical sensation of breath as it brushes the top of your nostrils as it moves in and moves out, while maintaining some awareness of the rest of your body sitting there . . . Let the breath move by itself while gently resting your awareness on the breath . . . rest in the breath as it moves in and moves out . . . When you notice that your mind is wandering, bring your awareness to those thoughts (realize what you are thinking) and then label the thoughts THINKING and return gently and lovingly back to your breath. Return your awareness to the breath . . .

Sit in this awareness of breath for ten minutes. Then take a couple of deep breaths and go about your day.

Training the Mind: Lojong

Lojong is an ancient Tibetan Buddhist practice designed to open your heart to your life and awaken your trust. *Lojong* literally means "mind training." The intent of the practice is to offer practical techniques

"If someone comes along and shoots an arrow into your heart, it's fruitless to stand there and yell at the person. It would be much better to turn your attention to the fact that there's an arrow in your heart and to relate to that wound."

—PEMA CHÖDRÖN, TIBETAN NUN, AUTHOR OF *START WHERE YOU ARE*

"Impulses, hunches, sudden insights and subtle insights have assisted us on our evolutionary path since the origin of our species."

—GARY ZUKAV, AUTHOR OF *THE SEAT OF THE SOUL*

that help you to cultivate more tenderness and compassion, loosening the grip of any negative thoughts and behaviors and using everyday experiences as your opportunity to awaken spiritually. Fundamental to this practice are fifty-nine slogans organized under seven headings, or "points"—thus, "The Seven Points of Mind Training." These slogans are succinct one-liners that help train your mind (and heart) to be more compassionate toward yourself and others.

These ancient affirmations are applied as reminders of how to think and behave. The slogans are pointers to guide you to the truth about you. You are not meant to shout them at yourself or to repeat them as if they were demands. Consider them a guide to the truth, to what really is possible for you. Don't use them to beat yourself over the head. What good would that do? Use them as gentle reminders, the same way you might remind yourself to brush your teeth or to send someone a birthday card. (To learn more about the slogans refer to Pema Chödrön's book *Start Where You Are* and Chögyam Trungpa's book *Mind Training*.)

The following slogan is especially appropriate for developing self-confidence, because it encourages you to always trust your own truth.

Slogan Number 20: "Of the two witnesses, trust the principal one."

This slogan reminds you that you really are the "principal" witness, especially when it comes to yourself. Who knows better what you like and don't like? Who knows better what is good for you and what isn't? Who knows better your fears and hopes? You are the one person who will accompany yourself throughout your life. You are the one witnessing everything that happens inside and outside of you. So when peers or adults are giving you their opinions and ideas, which may be good to listen to and consider, be sure to listen to your own truth. Don't go along with someone else's idea simply to gain approval or to be more popular or accepted—choose it because it feels right to you. The real witness, the one who really knows what you need and want, is you—so listen to yourself.

To use this slogan, simply hold it in your consciousness and apply its truth as much as possible in your daily experiences. Use this slogan along with your energy body's wisdom to build trust in yourself. Notice how ideas and suggestions from others feel in your body. Do you feel loose and comfortable with this other person's idea, or tight and tense? You are the only one who knows if you are willing to try something new or are not open to it yet.

Trusting yourself means being willing to actually listen to yourself and being honest with yourself. If you are lying to yourself, then you will find it very difficult to trust yourself. Remember, energy always tells the truth—so listen honestly to what your wisdom body tells you.

 A Chicken or an Eagle

Your beliefs about yourself can limit you or empower you. No matter what someone else believes about you, it only matters if you believe it about yourself. What do you believe about yourself? What do others see when they look at you? Are you a chicken or an eagle? . . .

A man found an eagle's egg in the nest of a backyard hen. The eaglet hatched with the brood of chicks and grew up with them.

All his life the eagle did what the backyard chickens did, thinking he was a backyard chicken. He scratched the earth for worms and insects. He clucked and cackled. And he would often thrash his wings and fly a few feet into the air.

Years passed and the eagle grew very old. One day he saw a magnificent bird far above him in the cloudless sky. It glided in graceful

"Our journey of making friends with ourselves is not a selfish thing. We're not trying to get all the goodies for ourselves. It's a process of developing loving-kindness and a true understanding for other people as well."
—PEMA CHÖDRÖN, TIBETAN NUN, *THE WISDOM OF NO ESCAPE*

majesty among the powerful wind currents, with scarcely a beat of its strong golden wings.

The old eagle looked up in awe. "Who's that?" he asked.

"That's the eagle, the king of the birds," said his neighbor. "He belongs to the sky. We belong to the earth—we're chickens."

So the eagle lived and died a chicken, for that's what he thought he was.

—TRADITIONAL STORY FROM *STORIES OF THE SPIRIT,*
STORIES OF THE HEART, EDITED BY CHRISTINA FELDMAN
AND JACK KORNFIELD

"Journeys bring power and love
back into you. If you can't go somewhere,
move in the passageways of the self.
They are like shafts of light,
always changing, and you change
when you explore them."

—RUMI,
SUFI MASTER AND POET

"We have not come here to take prisoners,
But to surrender ever more deeply
To freedom and joy.
We have not come into this exquisite world
To hold ourselves hostage from love.
Run like hell my dear,
From anything
That may not strengthen
Your precious budding wings.
Run like hell my dear,
From anyone likely
To put a sharp knife
Into the sacred, tender vision
Of your beautiful heart."

—HAFIZ, SUFI MASTER, FROM *THE GIFT*

5

Psychic Protection
Self-Defense for Your Soul

◎ DAVID'S STORY ◎

Due to his mother's mental illness and chronic alcoholism, David was placed in foster care at an early age. He was one of the fortunate ones and ended up in a decent home. A place he cherished. Yet, as all children do, he loved and missed his mother and wished for her to get well so his family could live together again. When David was ten years old, his mother recovered long enough to regain custody of him and his sister. For a while, life was relatively normal. David attended school, hung out with friends after school, and came home to his mother and sister. However, it wasn't long before they were living on the street. David and his sister were not attending school, and they spent their days taking the bus with their mother to the temporary cleaning jobs that she took to pay for her cigarettes, alcohol, and some food. It was a crazy, sleepless life.

But David loved his mother, and still wanted to live with her.

Then one day as he was riding the bus with his mother and sister to yet another place, David suddenly jumped out of his seat and ran out the open back door of the bus onto the street. He continued to run, not knowing why or where he was going. It was not something he had thought about or planned—something inside of him pushed him off the bus and told his feet to run—just run. As he ran he thought, "I can't do this anymore . . . I can't stay."

His mother grabbed his sister and chased down a taxicab and caught up with David. She told the driver to take them to the local hospital, where she tried to convince the doctors to admit her son "because he is crazy!" But the doctors quickly recognized that it was not David who needed to be hospitalized. They placed his mother in an alcohol detox program and sent David and his sister back to the foster home.

David was safe again—missing his mother, but safe.

When he tells this story now he shares that it was "pure intuition" that saved him. His jumping off the bus and running was beyond reason and thought. He simply trusted that voice in him that said "No more," and ran: "If I had thought about it at all, I would not have done it. As a ten-year-old it was too difficult to think about leaving my mother."

Later in his teen years the same voice rescued him from another attempt to live a life with his mother. Again he wanted his family together, but again his mother soon began drinking and acting crazy. If he had thought much about it, he would have tried to hide the bottles again, try to make dinners for the three of them, and stay out of the way of his mother's boyfriends. He considered dropping out of school to take care of his mother and sister. Instead, that same inner push that made him run from the bus got him to call for help. One night, without thinking, he just got up from watching television and called social services to come pick up his sister and him. As they left with the social worker, he remembers telling his mother, "We will be back," and he really thought they would be. It was as if someone else had made the phone call for him. From then on, he stayed with his foster parents and succeeded in getting his high school diploma.

". . . perhaps all the dragons of our lives are princesses who are only waiting to see us once beautiful and brave."
—RAINER MARIA RILKE, GERMAN POET

⊚ THE STORY OF HALF-BOY ⊚
Borneo story, translated by
Michael Meade, storyteller and author

In this story it is told that Half-boy is born, a boy with only the right half of his body. Of course, he is unhappy and feels desperately incomplete. He becomes a constant source of irritation, embarrassment, and confusion for his family and the entire village. Nevertheless, he grows. That is to say, the half of him that can be seen grows. Eventually, he reaches the age of adolescence and puberty. His halfness and incompleteness become unbearable to him. His pain grows more evident and more troublesome to everyone around him.

One day he leaves the village, dragging himself along the way a half-person drags himself through life. He drags along until he reaches a place where the road crosses a river. At that crossroad, he meets another youth who exists as only the left half, the other half of a person. Immediately, they move toward each other as if fated to join together. Surprisingly, when they reach each other, they begin to fight and roll in the dust. Eventually, they fall into the river. After a time, from the river there arises an entire youth with both sides joined together. Because he has been in the river and in a great struggle, he feels disoriented and doesn't know where he stands. Then, the new youth begins to walk toward a village that he sees before him.

As he enters the village, he sees an old man and asks: "Can you tell me where I am? I have been struggling and don't know where I have arrived at." The old man says: "You have arrived home. You are back in the village where you were born. Now that you have returned whole, everyone can begin the dance and celebration." A great dance and feast begins. Everyone in the village joins the dance, especially the Half-boy become whole.

"I'm never scared of anything. But my tummy is."

—PRESCHOOLER, FROM
A MONSTER IS BIGGER THAN 9,
EDITED BY CLAIRE ERICKSEN

In both of the preceding stories, a young man was compelled by an inner voice to take action to change the damaging conditions of his life. Each of you has an inner guardian that will pull you toward safety and wholeness in your life. That instinctive voice can rescue you. Sometimes it will tell you to run to safety; sometimes it will tell you to quietly stay put until help arrives. It may move you to speak up in some situations, while in others it will warn you to keep still. Recognizing and reinforcing that inner protector is a powerful tool to help yourself in difficult times, whether the difficulty is due to an alcoholic parent, feeling incomplete, or suffering from stress at school.

Shamanic cultures taught their teenagers how to find wholeness and maintain their physical and psychic safety. This chapter offers you many simple yet powerful ways to protect that "tender vision of your beautiful heart."

WHOLENESS IS SAFETY

Being half of what you are, of what you are meant to be, is not safe for you. Becoming who you are—becoming *whole*—makes you strong, makes you safe, even when the world around you is not safe. In this time of transitioning from childhood to adulthood you need to find out what makes you whole, what helps you express your true nature. Listen to the words of Emerson, the great naturalist and author:

"Oh Man! There is no planet, sun or star could hold you, if you but knew who you are."

Wholeness Meditation

This mediation is particularly helpful for those of you who feel like the Half-boy, incomplete in some way. But it is also appropriate for any teenager, still "putting yourself together," in search of your adult half. Give yourself about five minutes to do this meditation and another five to journal your experiences. Have someone slowly read this aloud. You can do this medi-tation alone or in a group.

Find a quiet place and ground yourself.

With your eyes closed, imagine yourself in a place in nature that you enjoy. It could be in a field, on a mountainside, in a city park, or near a body of water—whatever place brings you a sense of safety and peace. Feel your body in this place; imagine the smells and sights that you would experience there. Look above you and see in the blue sky some soft white clouds floating by . . .

Now, imagine looking around you and finding a path . . . Begin walk-ing on this path. Walk down the path, simply noticing what might appear . . . Breathe and relax, and continue walking down the path.

As you continue to walk down the path, you notice an object of some kind on the path ahead. As you continue walking toward this object, you see that it is some kind of container. This is a sacred container that holds knowledge just for you. It may be a box or a bowl of some kind; it could be a bag or chest. It could even be a large hole in the ground. As you approach it, take notice of what material it is made of, its color, texture, and shape, and any decoration it may have.

When you reach this sacred container, sit down next to it.

Choose something to leave behind that is weighing you down or keeping you from feeling whole. Leave anything that is making life diffi-cult for you right now next to your sacred container. What worry, concern,

"If your own energetic vibrations are balanced and in harmony, if your outlook is positive and life-enhancing, then you have a natural protection."

—JUDY HALL, PSYCHIC HEALER, AUTHOR OF *THE PRINCIPLES OF PSYCHIC PROTECTION*

person or object is somehow keeping you from feeling complete? Trust what comes and place that next to the sacred container. Breathe and relax for a few breaths. Notice what you are leaving behind, and what feelings this brings up. Feel the spaciousness you have created in your self and your life as a result of leaving some things behind.

Now ask this question: What is it I need now to make me more whole, more complete? Ask that you be given something that will help you, now, to be more complete. Sit for a moment with this prayer request . . . breathing and praying . . .

When you feel ready, open the container and look inside. Notice what is there for you—this particular object, image, thought, or emotion is the answer to your request. Trust what comes. Trust what first appears. Remain sitting, taking note of the object that is meant to help you, at this time, become more whole, more complete. Breathe . . .

Now place the object in the palm of your hand. If it is too large, use your imagination to shrink it so it will fit into the palm of your hand. Then imagine taking this object in your hand and placing in your heart. Once it is in your heart, get up and begin walking back up the path . . . walking back through the woods, with this object in your heart . . . walking up the path to the place in nature where you began.

When you get back sit, in that place for a moment. Look inside your heart and find the object you brought back with you. Then begin to notice the room you are now in by feeling your feet on the floor and your breath rising and falling in your body.

When you feel ready, open your eyes and look around you. Then take a moment to look inside your heart and find the object there, making sure that you did bring it back with you.

Take a few moments to journal your experience. What does this object mean to you? How might this thing help you be more complete? How does it feel to have left some worry behind?

"Clouds come from time to time—and bring a chance to rest from looking at the moon."

—BASHŌ,
JAPANESE HAIKU POET

"I couldn't see anything but a very deep black hole. I thought that I just wasn't able to imagine anything, but Julie recommended that I trust whatever came to me. So I went with the big black void, and put this in my heart. And when I came back and journaled I realized that this black hole was my anger. I was angry with so many people. Bringing it back in my heart and looking at it gave me a chance to really deal with this blackness.

"The first thing I did was drop out of debate class. I really hated it and every time I went I was just pissed off at everyone. I had stayed in the class because I thought my parents really wanted me to, and I thought they'd be upset when I dropped out. But they were cool about it. My debate teacher was upset with me for the remainder of my senior year, but I could deal with that. I did feel more whole doing what made sense for me."

—JASMINE, AGE 17

"I found an apple, and I am not sure what it means . . . I guess it means health, and that maybe I need to take care of myself better."

—SCOTT, AGE 18

"Every time I do this journey my sacred container is a tree. And there is a large opening in the tree where advice and knowledge are kept for me. This tree feels very real to me—a place I can go to when I need help. Which is often."

—CAITLIN, AGE 18

"I left behind my car! I was so worried about my new car getting scratched and dented, it was really bad. It felt great to leave it there and not to be worried about it anymore."

—JAMES, AGE 18

CAN LOVE MAKE YOU WHOLE?

It is important to mention here that feeling incomplete is part of the journey through your teen years. To "come of age" means to meet up with your missing half, becoming a whole adult. However, many of us go in search of other things—fame, money, or romance—and in doing so lose sight of ourselves.

For teenagers this often means searching for the perfect relationship—the ultimate love partner. This is a very powerful drive during your teen years, and can remain so throughout your life. Unfortunately, many of us get lost on our way to find wholeness and happiness—we get lost in search of the perfect *Other* instead of seeking our whole and true self. Searching for someone else, rather than seeking your own wholeness, can create great difficulty for you and sometimes even endanger you.

Vija got quite lost. He felt so strongly about finding the right girl that he often forgot about himself. He would get so involved in his girlfriends' lives that he would forget his schoolwork, neglect his friends, and even forget to eat if a girlfriend was having problems. And he seemed to hook up with girls who were having a lot of difficulty themselves.

His latest girlfriend, Sophia, was a brilliant, attractive seventeen-year-old who was addicted to alcohol and marijuana. She would also do other drugs when she had the money. Vija tried to keep her clean and would succeed at it for a while but something would always pull Sophia back into her old habits. The last time this happened she actually hurt some of her friends in a drunk driving accident.

She was placed on probation, her driver's license was suspended, and the court ordered her to get counseling. Vija was hopeful that she would finally get her act together. But she quit counseling as

"In all the great spiritual and mystery traditions, the central theme, the guiding passion, is the deep yearning for the Beloved of the soul."

—JEAN HOUSTON, AUTHOR OF *THE SEARCH FOR THE BELOVED*

soon as the court order had been satisfied. Then the couple got pregnant and decided to move into Vija's parents' house.

What do you think happened to Vija's plans and dreams? Do you think that he found his other half in this relationship? Even Vija is unsure of what his dreams are at this time.

When you depend on a romantic relationship to make you feel okay or whole, you can get into trouble—sometimes big trouble. Rushing into what turns out to be a bad relationship can have painful consequences, and sometimes change the entire course of your life. Although your teen years are a great time to explore relationships, they are also an important time to explore *yourself*. To find *your* missing pieces, to focus on becoming whole. Yet often in our most difficult times, instead of seeking truth and strength within ourselves, we look for a romance to rescue us. Consider Rachel's story.

Rachel came to me because she was having a difficult time at home. Her father was very controlling and unwilling to compromise. Her mother kept saying that she was going to get a divorce but it never seemed to happen. There was always a crisis going on at home. Neither of her parents had money for Rachel's college education and they were unable to help her apply for schools. She was not well prepared for life after high school, but she insisted she was going to leave the house the moment she turned eighteen. When she came to me, she was in her senior year of high school and she was doing okay in her classes. However, she was overwhelmed because she committed herself to too many projects. When we talked about it, she said she didn't want to drop anything because being busy gave her a reason to stay away from home and to not focus on her worries.

A couple of months after she turned eighteen, in the beginning of her senior year, Rachel followed through on her promise, and during another crisis at home she got up and left. She found a place to live at

a friend's house but she felt she was a burden to her friend. When she came in to see me that week she said she felt "numb." She had recently ended a relationship with a boy she'd been seeing for three years. She told me she was overwhelmed and not sure what the future held for her. It was almost too much to focus on applying to colleges.

In my office I have I Ching cards one can use to ask questions and tune in to one's own inner truth. When it was time for Rachel to consult the cards, I was thinking she would want to know what she could do to calm the stress down, or to find a place to live, or what she might focus on to open up her life more to her future. Instead, she inquired about a young man she was having strong feelings for, and what she might do to get his attention. With so much to resolve in her life at that time, the last thing she needed was another relationship to deal with. Yet, it is understandable that at this troubled time she just wanted to feel loved, and to have something else to focus her emotions on. She just wanted *to feel connected to something greater* than all the difficulty surrounding her, and in our culture we are too often taught that this "thing" is a romantic partner.

Rachel had not been taught that spirit is with her *always* and that there are ways to tap into this greater power every day. The message she continually got from popular culture was that "happily ever after" always means finding "that guy" (or girl). Happily ever after *can* include romantic love but it *always* includes spirit. As Sobonfu Somé reminds us, "This world of spirit applies to absolutely everyone in the world. Because without spirit, we wouldn't even make it here. It would be really hard to know whether we were going to wake up tomorrow and be alive without spirit. It would be really hard to know we have life."

How well do you think Rachel would have dealt with all the decisions facing her if she got caught up in all the excitement and uncertainty of exploring a new romantic relationship? What kind of relationship do you think she would have had if she got involved with someone at this point in her life?

"Separation from spirit, as we see here in the West, causes a greater emphasis on romantic love. It creates a vortex of longing for another person, for another way of connecting. Yet, romantic love is only one way of finding that other connection, which is to spirit, that we are actually looking for."

—SOBONFU SOMÉ, AFRICAN SHAMAN,
AUTHOR OF *THE SPIRIT OF INTIMACY*

It's not that romantic love isn't wonderful—it can be. But it is really the desire to feel your place in this world, to have a sense of who you are, to be connected to spirit, that often drives you to connect with others romantically. In many traditions such as Sufism, sacred psychology, Buddhism, and mystical Christianity, the search for romantic love (for the Beloved) is recognized as our search for the sacred.

Consider the story of the Half-boy. If he had gone in search of romantic love rather than himself, where would he be now?

We all want to feel this sacred connection to something beautiful. Romantic love can make you feel like you have everything you could ever want. But soon you find out that even when you have found your "soul mate," after a while that yearning for the connection with more, with your purpose, with spirit, comes back. So, *romantic love is just part of finding wholeness and happiness.* Shamans know this to be true, and that is why they teach their youth about energy and spiritual power. Only from a place of spiritual empowerment can you call to you a romantic partner with whom you can truly be happy.

Once you devote yourself to being whole, you can more easily and successfully create healthy, safe relationships with others. Most of your life happens in relationships—with family, friends, teachers, neighbors, employers, acquaintances. Many of these relationships will be a source of great pleasure and even joy. But sometimes they will be difficult, causing stress and threatening your self-esteem. When this happens, you have the tools within yourself to be safe. You have the ability to protect yourself in all your relationships and situations.

WHAT IS PSYCHIC PROTECTION?

Psychic protection is the ability to create a safe place within and around yourself, so you can freely *be* yourself. It is a shield you create to deflect the negative or unwanted thoughts and energy of others and to prevent you from losing your energy and self to other people or places. It is a psychic form of self-defense and has been used for thousands of years by shamans and everyday folk alike. Psychic protection works by strengthening your energy body to defend against any negative influences. For shamans, psychic protection includes calling on guardian spirits to help them when they do their psychic "journeys."

When Do You Need Psychic Protection?

Everyone at some time or another needs psychic protection. In this busy, full, sometimes frantic world we live in, we are frequently exposed to negative energies. The following list of questions will help you identify situations when you need psychic protection from these negative energies.

- Is it difficult for you to relax and be yourself?
- Do you at times feel overwhelmed at school?

"God, grant me the Serenity to accept the things I cannot change, courage to change the things I can, and the Wisdom to know the difference."

—*SERENITY PRAYER,*
REINHOLD NIEBUHR,
AMERICAN THEOLOGIAN

**"I am protected in front of me.
I am protected to the right of me.
I am protected behind me.
I am protected to the left of me."**

—FROM *THE TEEN SPELL BOOK,* BY JAMIE WOOD

- Is it hard for you to focus at school (but you can do so when you are alone)?
- Do you feel "dumped on" by others?
- Do you tend to feel down when a friend is down?
- Does school or any other place make you feel drained, tired, or weak?
- Do you feel overly sensitive to your environment?
- Are there places or people that make you feel useless or worthless?
- Do you ever feel "not yourself"?
- Do you feel as if you give a lot of your energy to others?
- Do you feel drained of energy after being around a certain person?
- Do you suffer from anxiety or panic attacks?
- Do you feel certain people or places "suck" your energy, leaving you tired?
- Are there people in your life who put you down?
- Do you abuse prescription or recreational drugs? (This includes alcohol.)

"Where there is pain, cures will be found. Where there is poverty, wealth will be supplied. Where there are questions, answers will be given. Spend less time worrying, and more time trusting."

—RUMI, SUFI MASTER AND POET

If you answered yes to two or more of the above, you would benefit from psychic protection, and you may want to take some extra time in this chapter.

You can begin with this simple technique that I use regularly when I am scared or simply worried. It is a call to your spiritual source to go before you and prepare your way, to make things safer for you, and to be ready to come to your aid. Simply make this declaration, out loud or to yourself:

Spirit goes before me and prepares my way.

After saying this declaration to yourself, *take some time to imagine* a powerful guardian or force going before you and making things better and safer for you. Hold this in your mind as you go to meet your difficulty—whatever it may be.

Such prayers of protection are found throughout all spiritual practices. Many Christians pray to Mother Mary or St. Jude for protection. In Egypt, over three thousand years ago, they prayed to the divine Mother, Isis, for protection. The power of such prayer is your ability to call on the energies and spirits of these beings to protect you. You then carry their energy with you into the world and into the environment where you need protection.

"If people call you stupid and that upsets you, then you are immediately under their spell because at some level you believe them."

—JOSÉ STEVENS AND LENA S. STEVENS, AUTHORS OF *SECRETS OF SHAMANISM*

Casting a Spell of Protection

In some traditions, a meditation such as the one that follows is considered an "empowerment," a way to empower yourself; in other traditions it might be thought of as a "spell"—a way to make a wish powerful enough to become a reality in your life. There are many names for the same undertaking—use the one that works for you. If you feel stronger by saying you are casting a spell, go for it; if you would rather feel you are empowering yourself, then so be it.

Color Shield Meditation

Find time when you can be alone in your room, undisturbed, for five minutes. Sit in a meditative posture with your eyes closed.

Imagine bringing a white or golden light down from above to surround you. Let this light surround you and feel it touch your skin, so that this glow of golden or white light seems to come from you.

Now imagine the color of the light changing slowly to each of the colors of the rainbow: orange, red, yellow, purple, blue, and green (not black or brown). Notice how each color feels to you and which one makes you feel most protected. When you find the color that makes you feel the safest and the most protected, keep that colored light glowing around you. Know that this light will go with you to surround and protect you in any difficult situation. As you open your eyes, continue to imagine the shield of light still surrounding you. Any time you need it, you can simply invoke this shield and it will appear around you for your protection in emotionally or socially challenging situations. This protection is primarily energetic, so it will not protect you physically.

The Glass Body

A compelling shamanic technique for protecting yourself in difficult situations is "shape shifting." Shape shifting is about *changing your energy body* to take on the particular energy of an animal. There are many reasons for practicing shape shifting—for protection, to experience an animal's medicine, or to enter another reality. Many of us experience shape shifting in dreams, where we may become a bird or change into several people. In my class I refer to the following technique of shape shifting as the "Glass Body," or the Gandhi approach to protection. This exercise is very helpful in situations when you are with another person who is in the habit of dumping on you and who usually leaves you feeling awful. (Even when someone has a reason to be mad at you, it doesn't give him or her the right to dump negativity on you.)

> *his words fell*
> *like rocks from his mouth*
> *and clattered all around him.*

"The ultimate nature of all human interactions is that they are exchanges of energy—positive exchanges, negative exchanges, neutral exchanges, but exchanges in one way or another."

—VICTOR SANCHEZ, MEXICAN SHAMAN, AUTHOR OF *THE TOLTEC PATH OF RECAPITULATION*

"Shamans often change their appearance (energetically) or disguise themselves in order to go undetected or avoid unwanted attention."

—JOSÉ STEVENS AND LENA S. STEVENS, AUTHORS OF *SECRETS OF SHAMANISM*

even after
the avalanche had cleared,
I could feel them jostling
around
in my head
keeping me awake.

—KIRSTEN SAVITRI BERGH, TEEN POET

Do this exercise a few minutes before you are about to have a face-to-face with someone who puts you down.

Take a moment to ground. Remember to relax and breathe. Now visualize an image of yourself standing before you. Picture yourself as a clear glass body. Then bring that glass body over to you and surround yourself with it. You are shape shifting, changing energetically into a glass body. Now go to meet the negative person, knowing that all through your interaction you will be present in a glass body. What this means is that any negativity aimed at you will just pass through you. Your energy body will follow Gandhi's example, not pushing against or resisting the other person's words, but simply letting them pass through you. You are neutral, unmoved by what is being said. Remember to breathe when you are with this person.

After the person has left, take a moment to check in with yourself. Are you feeling any negativity in your body or emotions? If so, it means that a particular comment made by this other person "stuck" to a belief inside you that the comment is true. When you are in the glass body, all the other person's negativity just moves through you

"The needle that pierces our hearts carries the thread that binds us to Heaven."

—JAMES HASTINGS, AUTHOR OF *THE ENCYCLOPEDIA OF RELIGION AND ETHICS*

"Light is always stronger than darkness, and that silver lining can take over an entire gray, billowing cloud—if only you will believe it can."

—JAMIE WOOD, AUTHOR OF *THE TEEN SPELL BOOK*

and can only get stuck on a place in you that agrees to it. Your glass body is like a clean window—all the light shines through it, only getting stuck on any dust or dirt that may remain on the window. So when Joe says, "You are worthless," if *you* don't believe this to be true about yourself, his energy and comment will just past right through your glass body. If you *do* already believe this about yourself, you will feel his negative comment in your physical and energy body. This is a signal that you need to examine this belief and begin to work through why you believe it and what you can do about making it *untrue* for you.

Tamara, a seventeen-year-old client, once asked, "How is it that I can have a great day until just one person gives me a bad look or says something nasty to me? Everything good that happened to me the rest of the day gets trashed!"

This can be true for many of us—and there is one reason this typically happens. You get brought down because that nasty look or comment hooks up with *a belief or perception you hold of yourself* that is dormant—not in your conscious awareness. If it didn't feel true to you somehow, it wouldn't be likely to bother you. When you feel brought down as a result of what someone has said to you, or how someone has acted toward you, it is time to check in with yourself. Ask yourself: *What belief in me agrees with this person's negative take on me?*

When you do identify a negative belief about yourself, examine it with an open and relaxed mind. Is this belief based on unfair and untrue criticisms that you have heard all your life? Or, underneath the unnecessary harshness and negativity, is there a germ of truth in it? If you determine that the belief is someone else's voice that you have carried too long, now it is time to banish it from your life. If you sense that there is some truth to this belief, you need to decide how

"Even from a dark night songs of beauty may be born."

—Maryanne Radmacher-Hershey, American author

"Earth and heaven are in us."

—Mahatma Gandhi, Indian pacifist leader

you want to handle it. You may decide that this aspect of yourself is something you are ready to change. If so, you can begin to make a realistic and positive plan for what you will need in order to make that change (see A Model for Changing on page 212). If, instead, you recognize that this is a part of you that you cannot change, or are not yet ready to change, you need to be kind to yourself and acknowledge that you, like everyone else, are human and not perfect. You *still* have every right to feel safe and good about yourself.

Five Differences

Another simple, in-the-moment strategy for protecting yourself in a negative encounter with someone is to focus on identifying five physical differences between you and the other person. Simply name these five differences to yourself. "Jane has blue eyes and I have green. She is taller than I am. I sing in the choir and she does not." This helps you to be in your own space and to successfully differentiate yourself from the other person. You are less likely to take on her stuff, her negative energy, when you take control of your thoughts this way. I find it gives me something else to "listen" to instead of the criticism or the blaming that the other person may be engaging in. It also helps keep your energy neutral because you are not automatically reacting to the energy of what the other person is communicating to you.

Clearing Out Negative Energy

Are there times when you feel you just can't shake a negative feeling? Or, after being with a certain person, do you always feel down? Often this occurs after someone has "attacked" you with negative energy. He or she may not have *said* anything, but instead attacked you nonverbally—just giving you *that look* and zapping you energetically. Being more aware of the energy world will help you realize when this has happened. Then, you can do something about it and not carry this harmful energy around.

When energy is hurled at you, there will usually be some harm to your energy body. Therefore, you will need to release that negative energy. Crying, talking about it, and *breathing* are natural and effective ways to release that energy, as are all the breathing practices in this book. The following exercise can be especially helpful to free yourself of the negative energy you take on from others.

Amethyst Rain Meditation

Give yourself about five to ten minutes for this exercise. Take a moment to ground and sit comfortably but alert in a chair with your feet on the floor. Take five deep breaths through the nose, holding for a moment and then releasing through the mouth. On each exhale imagine releasing the negativity from your body.

On the next inhale, while relaxing in the breath, visualize an amethyst cloud above you. Watch this cloud shower amethyst raindrops on you and right through you. Continue to breathe, taking nice deep breaths through the nose and exhaling through the mouth. Imagine every cell, every molecule and atom being washed by this rain of amethyst . . . the lavender water cleansing you and going down into the earth where it can be recycled and reused. Stay with this image for as long as you need to.

Hoocha Meditation

This meditation comes from the Q'ero tradition of Brazil. The Q'ero people believe that there is a being, called Hoocha, in our bodies that will gobble up any negative and dark energy we have in our selves. At the end of each day people will take the time to let Hoocha clear out any negativity that they are carrying in their physical and energetic bodies. They understand the importance of not holding on to the negative energy of others.

Give yourself five minutes alone in your room sometime before you go to sleep at night. Focus your attention on the bottom of the second chakra (below your belly button). Now imagine Hoocha there. He has a big mouth that is opening and beginning to eat all the dark, negative energy in your body. Imagine the darkness being consumed by this being, his jaws crunching and his throat gulping. Like water in a plastic bottle with a hole in the bottom, the negativity begins to empty out of you, moving down from your head to your second chakra, where the Hoocha consumes it. Any of the "crumbs" that fall to the side go out the bottoms of your feet into the earth.

When the Hoocha has eaten all the negativity in you, he will close his eyes and fall asleep smiling. When he does, sit for a moment, breathing and enjoying the freshness of your energy body.

Opening the Soul's Window

Here is another quick clearing technique that can be used any time you find you are carrying a negative thought or feeling. Simply ask

yourself, *Is this* my *feeling? Is this* my *thought?* Just ask the question. When you ask yourself something like this, you are screening and filtering your feelings, not allowing yourself to just take in and *assume* negativity. The question opens the door inside your soul; like opening a window in the house, this brings in fresh air. You don't have to force an answer, or even think about the answer—just ask yourself the question: *Is this my stuff?* Your soul will help you answer the question. So often we just go around carrying all this negativity that isn't really ours, without asking, *Whose stuff is this anyway?* Once the window to the soul is open, once the fresh air is let in, your soul steps in, and behind the scenes (without your knowing it) helps clear out what isn't yours. Keeping your mind alert by asking such questions is a very powerful tool for psychic protection.

Spirit Helpers and Allies

Shamans and many other spiritual teachers regularly call on the spirit world for help. They identify specific spirit guardians and allies to accompany them on their spiritual journeys for guidance and protection. Shamans also draw strength from the natural world, calling on the power of animals, rocks, and plants.

Perhaps you can benefit from seeking a guardian from the spirit world or from nature. Do you already have a sense of a guardian angel, or perhaps a deceased grandparent or pet that is with you, protecting and supporting you? Are you especially fond of certain animals, such as turtles, bears, or hawks? Notice which animals you surround yourself with (look at your stuffed animals, jewelry, or posters). One of them is probably a power animal for you.

By calling on spirit helpers and allies you can empower yourself when you feel the need for protection. Invite them, whoever they are, to walk beside you. Invite a bear or other animal, Jesus, the

"Grandfather, Great Spirit, . . . You have seen the powers of the four quarters of the earth to cross each other. You have made me cross the good road, and the road of difficulties, and where they cross, the place is hot. Day in, day out, forevermore, you are the life of things."
—BLACK ELK, OGLALA SIOUX ELDER

"Stop. I see something. Far away there is a flash of fire.
You did not see me . . .
A fox bounces brightly through the bush."
—KOYUKON RIDDLE

Buddha, Saint Christopher, Padmasambhava, your guardian angel, your grandfather who loved you, or the Great Goddess to stand by your side as you confront a difficult or challenging situation. Because *energy is real and holds power,* the presence of your allies will be felt by you and by others as well. You will notice an increase in personal power and courage when you call on your allies.

To call on your allies, you can be standing or sitting. Begin as always by grounding and taking a couple of deep breaths. Then tell your allies why it is you need their help, and invite them to join you. Imagine them (or him or her) standing next to you or surrounding you. Ask them to accompany you into your difficult situation. As you walk toward your destination, imagine them walking by your side or behind you. I often call on Padmasambhava, the Buddha of compassion, and my power animal, the red-tailed hawk, to accompany me.

I have a friend who brought an ally with him to his first job after college. He was a social worker in a stressed and sometimes perilous neighborhood. He would have to show up to work in the evening hours when the streets were often full of people who were drugged and drunk. In order to feel (and be) stronger and safer, he brought with him his bear ally. He would call on his big black bear to walk right behind him, providing courage and protection for him as he walked from his car to the building where he worked. He did this every night for several months.

Then one day he was called in to work early. Because the sun was still shining and the streets were quieter, he felt safer and forgot to call on his bear ally before he left home.

As my friend approached the building a homeless man lay huddled in a corner keeping warn. The man looked up at my friend and asked him, "Where's the bear?"

Your ally too will be felt, and perhaps even seen, by others. Try it out some day when you are afraid or simply need that extra support.

"I use my ally when I want to stand up for myself. I think others do sense my ally, or can feel something different about me."

—JAKE, AGE 19

You may also want to invite your friends or living elders to be present as your allies in times when you are dealing with difficult people or situations. You never have to be alone at such times. Any time you feel unsafe, take an ally with you. Don't allow yourself to be ganged up on, by peers, teachers, or any adult in authority. Ask your parents or another adult who believes in you to be with you.

"My boss called me in to a 'meeting' after I told him I was leaving my job. I knew he was going to dump on me, big time! I told him that I was going to bring my older brother to the meeting. My employer said that there was no need for that, but I told him I was going to anyway. So he canceled the meeting."

—ANNETTE, AGE 19

"Stand in the Light when you want to speak out."
—CROW PROVERB

YOU ARE THE LIGHT

Shamans know that our intentions, our motives and reasons for doing things, hold great power. That is why prayers, affirmations, chants, and meditations are so effective; they express our *intentions*. In fact, every prayer, expectation, hope, and chant is an *intention*. My spiritual teacher continually reminded us that "energy follows intention"—

intentions put out their own energy. Your intentions have the power to attract and to create. In the following prayer you are sending out the intention of protection and truth:

I am the Light
The Light is within me
The Light moves throughout me
The Light surrounds me
The Light protects me
I am the Light.

As you repeat this prayer, imagine the light within you, moving through you, surrounding and protecting you. Feel the light lifting and strengthening you. Focus your thoughts on the above intention and the intention becomes real. This prayer reminds you of who you truly are—a being of energy, of light.

"I will not die an unlived life.
I will not live in fear
of falling or catching fire.
I choose to inhabit my days,
to allow my living to open me,
to make me less afraid,
more accessible;
to loosen my heart
until it becomes a wing,
a torch, a promise.
I choose to risk my significance,
to live so that which came to me as seed
goes to the next as blossom,
and that which came to me as blossom,
goes on as fruit."

—DAWN MARKOVA, FROM
"I WILL NOT LIVE AN UNLIVED LIFE"

Anything Is Possible
Your Creative Power

◎ 6

◎ JULIA'S SECRET BOX ◎

Julia lived in an abusive, hostile environment. Both her parents emotionally abused her. They would belittle her and tell her she was going to fail at anything she attempted. But, as you will see in her story, Julia had a secret that kept her creative spirit safe and alive.

I started filling my box when I was in seventh grade. It's really just an old ammo box that I used as a pencil box when I still drew portraits and landscapes in what precious playtime I had. I hid this box under my bed. My parents were not exactly supportive when it came to anything I did. They belittled me for my art. They said that I would never amount to anything if I kept up my drawing, and, being twelve, I believed them and quit.

Their taunts did not quit with my drawing. I was the chosen target for all of their frustrations. They decided that I was a "useless bitch," and they never passed up an opportunity to remind me of this whenever they got the chance, and as I got older the name calling got worse though the physical abuse was tapering off. Being called worthless by your own family hurts more than any beating.

At a particularly low point, just after I had tried to take my own life, I transformed my box. It became my "bible." In it I put everything that I held dear. It didn't take long to fill it with pretty stones, seashells, dead bugs, foreign money, small toys, and printed stories of ancient wisdom that I found fascinating. The box became an extension of my soul. While I had to change on the outside to cope with my life, my box contained my true self. In my box my "tender heart" still beat and I still loved the natural world and its beauty. While I became stoic, cynical, and sarcastic, my box held my soul for safekeeping.

I hid my box in various places to protect it . . . hiding my heart from the hell that was my life. When things got bad, I would bring out the box. It was a source of strength for me . . . my empowerment. Once, my mother found my box, and with her critical eye examined its contents and declared it the "dumbest thing" she'd ever seen. Her comment cut deep into my heart. That box held the essence of who I am. She criticized my soul when she criticized my box.

I declared my independence that day. I would get away from that place, and I would start my own life and be my own person. I would not have to hide my heart in a box under my bed. By that time, the box was the center of my universe. I was older then, and getting ready to go to college. I taped a bumper sticker from my college to the lid and began counting down the days. Whenever I opened the box I was reminded of my ultimate goal. Finally, the morning I left for college, I packed my box.

As I write this, Julia is in her second year of college. She is on the honor roll and volunteers as a Girl Scout leader to local impoverished girls. She teaches them how to make candles out of beeswax, draw and paint, and believe in themselves through their art.

"No one is hurt by doing the right thing."

—HAWAIIAN PROVERB

"I have thousands of books in my brain. I can tell you anything."

—LYDIA ISHMAEL, AGE 6

"Human salvation lies in the hands of the creatively maladjusted."

—MARTIN LUTHER KING JR., CIVIL RIGHTS LEADER

 Ancient Tibetan Story
retold by Julie Tallard Johnson

There was once a famous Tibetan medicine man who was revered by everyone for his healing powers. He was particularly gifted at chanting mantras. Many would come and listen to him. Students would travel great distances to receive spiritual instructions from this great teacher.

One day this great Lama was out canoeing on a large lake when he heard a man chanting on a distant island. As he got closer he heard the chant that very few sing because it is so difficult and is meant to be sung so precisely. This particular chant, when done correctly, is said to bring the chanter enlightenment and such powers as walking on water and healing the sick. Well, this chanter was singing it wrong. The Lama, having a kind heart, got off his boat and gently tapped the lone chanter on the shoulder. "Excuse me, kind sir, but you are doing the chant incorrectly."

The chanter recognized the great Lama and was both surprised and pleased. "Oh, thank you for letting me know. I have been out here for months and months chanting. Could you please teach me the right way to do this chant?" The great Lama took several weeks to teach this dedicated young man the right way to sing the chant. On the final day, the great Lama decided the man had the chant down perfectly and left him to chant alone on the island. The young man was very grateful for this help.

As the great Lama paddled away, he could hear the young man chanting. He sounded beautiful and the Lama was happy that the chant was being sung correctly. But then he heard the chanter return to the way he had been chanting before the Lama had taught him. And it was all wrong. As the Lama listened he saw something crossing over the water approaching him. It was first just a black spot on the lake but as it got closer the Lama knew what it was.

The young man, having walked across the water, tapped on the Lama's shoulder and asked, "How did the chant go again?"

"Every time you don't follow your inner guidance, you feel a loss of energy, loss of power, a sense of spiritual deadness."

—Shakti Gawain, author of *Developing Intuition*

OPENING UP TO YOUR SHAKTI

*"I learned that the real creator was
my inner Self, the Shakti . . .
That desire to do something is
God inside talking through us."*

—MICHELE SHEA,
INSPIRATIONAL SPEAKER AND WRITER

"The creative person is the master rather than the slave of his imagination."

—MICHAEL LEBOEUF, FROM *IMAGINEERING*

"Nothing is as real as a dream. The world can change around you, but your dream will not. Responsibilities need not erase it. Duties need not obscure it. *Because the dream is within you,* no one can take it away."

—TOM CLANCY, NOVELIST

You are directly connected to the creative power of the universe—it is inside you; it surrounds you and connects you to all things. It is always available to you. This creative energy that is inside of you is called the *shakti*. The shakti, according to yogic tradition, is the female energy of the soul, which is the original source of all creative energy and ideas, the energy that gives birth to your ideas. Your shakti is the embodiment of creative power. All you have to do is tap in to this energy and you will bring about good things. This creative energy inside of you will connect with the energy outside of you—and make things happen!

At the center of many spiritual practices, you will find the importance of creative expression. This is because each of us is meant to *create*. Spirit wants us to create. Shamanic practices teach you to harness the powers of your imagination in order to manifest your dreams. You have inside of you this fire, this shakti, this desire to be something, to create, to become. Listening to this shakti, feeling its burn, is listening to the voice of spirit, of the creator, talk to you and through you. When you are in touch with this creative fire inside of you, you will know that there are things you are meant to do, "riches" you are meant to share.

"Our deepest desire is to share our riches, and this desire is rooted in the dynamics of the cosmos. What began as an outward expansion of the universe in the fireball ripens into your desire to flood all things with goodness. Whenever you are filled with a desire to fling your gifts into the world, you have become this cosmic dynamic of celebration, feeling its urgency to pour forth just as the stars felt the same urgency to pour themselves out."

—THOMAS BERRY, POET

Your "riches" may be offbeat and unconventional; they may even disturb some people. Only you can truly know what form your shakti will take. Discovering just how your creative expression will manifest will be a primary focus during your teen years and into your twenties.

There is a saying that there are many paths to the Buddha's house—many roads to enlightenment and happiness. There is not just *one way* to bring forth your intuitive and creative powers. The young man in the Tibetan story was doing the chant "wrong," yet he was able to walk on water. We are told to color inside the lines but often the hand of the most creative child goes outside the lines. Creativity is messy. Creativity is a surprise. Creativity is dynamic and personal. Your creativity is an expression of your very soul and its connection to spirit. There is no wrong or right way to be creative. Sometimes we have to hide our creativity from insulting words, sometimes we may want to create a special place to hold our creative dreams.

CREATE YOUR OWN SACRED BOX

If you are in a situation similar to Julia's, you may want to create your own sacred box. It can be as simple as a shoe box. You may

"To live the creative life we must lose our fear of being wrong."

—JOSEPH CHILTON PEARCE, AUTHOR OF *THE CRACK IN THE COSMIC EGG*

"Desire, ask, believe, receive."

—STELLA TERRILL MANN, CHRISTIAN AUTHOR

want to decorate it. Whatever its shape or appearance, your sacred box will hold evidence of your true self—your creative self. It will remind you that spirit is active in your life. Fill it with cards that friends have given you, quotes that empower you, ideas that come to you, pictures of your allies. Place some of your favorite art in it. Collect objects that inspire you and give you hope during difficult times, and keep it in a place where you can look at it when you need to remind yourself of your dreams and who you really are. If school is more difficult for you than home, perhaps your box can be in your locker at school.

"There is a vitality, a life force, an energy, a quickening, that is translated through you into action, and because there is only one of you in all time, this expression is unique. And if you block it, it will never exist through any other medium and will be lost."

—MARTHA GRAHAM,
INFLUENTIAL DANCER AND
CHOREOGRAPHER

"I started a box because my parents don't get what it is I am all about. I want to leave the family business and find myself. Find out what is truly me. I feel bad about leaving my younger brother behind; he is going into middle school next year. But Julie says that going out and doing my life will be a better help to him than staying home. My box is filling up with stuff that keeps me focused—quotes from the Tao Te Ching, my best friend's picture, lyrics from favorite songs, some stones, a scholarship I was given, and a pamphlet about the college I will be attending. I want to be a music teacher when I graduate. When I am down and afraid nothing is really going to work out for me, I just look inside my box."

—SARAH, AGE 18

TO IMAGINE IS TO CREATE

Mark Twain was known for saying, "You can't depend on your judgment when your imagination is out of focus." And most of us have heard the saying attributed to the physicist Albert Einstein: "Imagination is more important than knowledge." It is your imagination that the shamans claim is your ultimate power in creating the life you want.

Creative Visualization

Creative visualization is a potent technique of imagining—"seeing"—things as you would *like* them to be in your life, so they can *become* real.

Shauna was very stressed about taking the college placement exams, which were a week away. She had studied for them and was doing well in school, but still she was becoming increasingly anxious.

Then she sat down and did a simple visualization in which she imagined doing well on her exams. She breathed and relaxed and used the visualization exercise to calm her fears. She "saw" herself going into the testing room and being focused and relaxed. She felt how it would be to have the energy and mind power to focus on four hours of exams. She imagined herself finishing up each exam in time and feeling very good about being done.

She practiced this visualization a few times the week before the tests. When she took the exams she found herself moving through all the questions effortlessly and not getting hung up on the ones she didn't know. She finished up with time to spare and felt great about the whole experience.

Without your imagination you cannot create anything or make anything happen in your life. This chapter shows you how you can use your imagination to manifest your dreams. Your ability to imagine something for yourself will increase what you will actually *have* in your life. If you can "see" it, you can create it.

"The world of reality has its limits; the world of imagination is boundless."
—JEAN-JACQUES ROUSSEAU, FRENCH PHILOSOPHER

"For shamans imagination encompasses more than just brain activity; a vital and principal vehicle, imagination connects us with the web of power and the spirit in all things."
—JOSÉ STEVENS AND LENA S. STEVENS, *SECRETS OF SHAMANISM*

Fantasy versus Imagination

There is a big difference between imagination and fantasy. Fantasy is what a gambling addict uses to justify a destructive habit. Fantasy is not real . . . is not grounded and often is not even safe. It is the voice that says, "I will feel better *when* . . . I am thin, or I win the lottery." Fantasy is not productive and is a displacement of your intention and creative energy. Whereas you want to be rich and successful, you end up using your energies to fantasize rather than using your imagination to create what you desire. Without *creative* use of the imagination, fantasy has no power to become a reality.

Fantasy is an illusion and doesn't *feel* authentic in the body. The energy of imagination and of fantasy are different. The more you practice listening to your body, the more you will know what is true and what is not—what is a creative idea and what is an illusion.

Try this: Find a lottery ticket and hold it in your hand. Take a moment to feel the energy of this ticket and the thoughts and beliefs it generates. Notice how you feel in your body. This is the energy of a *fantasy*—an illusion. Notice how your energy body feels after watching too much television. This is the energy of illusion and fantasy.

Now put the ticket down and imagine finishing a race or doing well on an exam, accomplishing something you have worked for. Imagine how you will feel at the finish line after weeks of training, or putting down your pencil when you've finished the exam that you studied so hard for. How does this feel in your body? Notice the difference in the energy. Imagination will feel more grounded, alive, and real, while fantasy will feel unreal and static.

Your Own Manifestation Bowl

Find a bowl that looks and feels right to you, or make a bowl if you are so inclined. This will be your personal manifestation bowl.

To use it, you first need to know what it is you want. Be as specific as possible (the vaguer you are, the less likely you are to get what you really want). Consider in detail what it is you would like to manifest in your life at this time.

Write it down on a small piece of paper. Fold up the paper and place it in the bowl. Hold the bowl in your hands and place your energy and your intention into the bowl. Feel around the bowl's edges; this is your personal manifestation tool. Put your love and energy into the entire bowl.

Now bring to mind that which you want to manifest. While holding on to your bowl with the paper in it, imagine this particular request coming true for you. Use your imagination to notice what the manifestation of your intention will look like, feel like, smell and taste like. Breathe . . . and imagine how your life will be with this particular request manifested. Take as much time as you need to get the full feel of having this request come true for you.

Then place the bowl in a special place in your home. This can be in an obvious place where you will easily see it every day or it may be in a private place just for you.

After a week, unfold the paper and read your request to yourself. Then burn it safely in a fire or by candlelight, letting it go out to the universe to bring forth that which you asked for.

All of our addictions (to food, drugs, alcohol, sex, relationships, television) are rooted in fantasy. The "white knight" or "beautiful princess" fantasy is a particularly alluring one. "If I can just find my white knight, all will be right in my world." José, who is now eighteen

years old and has a serious drug addiction problem, knows he needs help. But he keeps focusing his mind on finding the "perfect girl." He goes from one fantasy girl to the next, as his friends are getting jobs, moving on to college, and getting on with their lives.

Sometimes you may need help in believing you can make something happen. You may feel stuck, or afraid, or just unsure of yourself. Using a manifestation bowl (see page 163) and walking the spiral (below) are two ways to invite the creative energy inside you, your shakti, to connect with the creative force outside of you. Manifestation is a result of these two creative energies coming together through the use of your imagination. When you do these exercises, keep this thought in mind: That which you are searching for is also searching for you.

Walking the Spiral

The spiral is a shape that is plentiful in the natural world: in seashells, vegetables, and vines. It is an important symbol in many spiritual traditions. Its design expresses how everything is connected *and* that everything changes. No matter where you are in the spiral you are connected to every other part of the spiral. Its circular path represents cycles in nature such as the phases of the moon and the rising and falling of the tide. These cycles remind us that everything is always changing. The spiral also represents balance in life—you cannot live in one state of being all the time. You can't *always* be creating, or sleeping, or angry, or happy. You circle in and out of these emotions and states. The spiral helps you to get in touch with this natural and creative "flow."

In the wild prairie that sits outside our front door we have created a Sacred Spiral to walk. Many adults and teenagers have come to walk it, seeking advice. It is a path that circles in to a center. At

> "You are the artist, you are the raw material, you are the work of art and you are the reality behind the work of art . . . One experiences ecstasy when one discovers the creator in one, as oneself.
>
> "The whole of life is a process whereby the unmanifest becomes manifest. Divine Creativity is completed by human creativity. Of all the qualities in your being, the one that is most Godlike is creativity."
>
> —PIR VILAYAT INAYAT KHAN, SUFI MYSTIC

the center is an altar, a simple stone for offering prayers and blessings. To walk a spiral is a means to consult with the divine inside of you (your shakti) and outside of you (the creator, spirit, nature, the Tao). It connects you with your inner truths, and gives you an idea of where in the circle of life you may be at this moment. It can help you see what you need to move forward with confidence and purpose.

> *"I went into the spiral with the question about my own path. I turn eighteen in only a few months and I will have a summer to get my act together and figure out who I am. I realize it will take longer than that but I just want a first step. A sense of things. Julie asked me to identify and release my greatest fear before entering the spiral. I released the fear of getting lost. I am so afraid that somehow I will just get lost and never find out who I truly am and what my true path is. And since I am an agnostic I don't pray to any God. So I put out this prayer to myself and to the Tao, to help me release this fear.*
>
> *"Then I crossed over the threshold and began my walk into the center of the spiral. What really freaked me out was that I found myself at one point feeling really lost. But instead of tripping out totally, I waited a moment. I breathed and relaxed and took a minute to find myself and then finished my walk into and then out of the spiral. It was powerful."*
>
> —JAMIE, AGE (ALMOST) 18

Jamie's experience in the spiral provided her with a lot of insight. As she walked the spiral she had to face the very thing she most feared in her life—that she would get lost. But this time she moved through it and didn't let the fear get out of hand. Her feelings of being lost didn't stop her. Our souls communicate with us through such symbolic acts

"The range of what we think and do is limited by what we fail to notice."

—R. D. LAING,
BRITISH PSYCHIATRIST

"The universe is a fluid, ever-changing energy pattern, not a collection of fixed and separate things. What affects one thing affects, in some way, all things: All is interwoven into the continuous fabric of being. Its warp and weft are energy, which is the essence of magic."

—STARHAWK,
FROM *THE SPIRAL DANCE*

as walking the spiral, so she moved through her fear on a very deep, soul level. Chances are if this fear comes up for her in the day-to-day world, she will again just breathe and move through it. It may even be that she has successfully passed through the fear and will not experience it again. With fear no longer blocking her path, she can look ahead and imagine her future.

Peter, aged eighteen, walked the spiral and found a deep sense of peace when he was done. "I just felt more connected to myself and everything. I don't know how it will help, but I know it has somehow . . ."

Creating a Spiral Walk

Before creating your own spiral walk, you may first want to check with your local colleges, cathedrals, or Celtic and spiritual bookstores for the location of a sacred spiral near you. You can also contact Circle Sanctuary (circle@mhtc.com). They have a networking source book of groups who celebrate the earth by offering labyrinth and spiral walks to their communities. More resources are listed and described at the end of this book.

You can create a spiral walk inside or outside, although it is best if you can do this out-of-doors. This will connect you more directly with the natural rhythms of earth and sky. To create an outdoor spiral you can use rocks, cornmeal, or sticks to outline the path. You may even want to mow a path in an unmowed lawn or in a prairie. As a school or class project you can create a spiral or labyrinth on the school gym floor with chalk, paper, or objects such as books. Make it as large as possible with room in the center for an altar and room at the entrance for a threshold.

The threshold is the entrance to the spiral, a place where you acknowledge that you are leaving the mundane world and entering

"Energy flows in spirals. Its motion is always circular, cyclical, wavelike. The spiral motion is revealed in the shape of galaxies, shells, whirlpools, DNA."

—STARHAWK,
THE SPIRAL DANCE

"When the earth was made
When the sky was made
When my songs were first heard
The holy mountain was standing toward me with life."

—APACHE AFFIRMATION

the world of the sacred. A threshold can be made of special or sacred objects or it can be just a simple opening to the spiral. If the spiral is indoors, the threshold can be the door going into the room.

The author's sacred spiral

All spiritual traditions teach us that in very deliberately sending out our prayers and requests, we ignite a personal response from the spirit world. If you don't put an intention out there, it is much like an unsent letter. How do you expect to get a response? In sending a request out, how do you expect *not* to get a response? Likewise, if we never went to the mailbox to actually retrieve the response, it would be as if we never got one. If you *pay attention* on the way out of the spiral (and in the weeks after your spiral walk), you will then notice a response.

"The Sacred dance is circular."

—BARBARA G. WALKER, AUTHOR OF *THE WOMAN'S DICTIONARY OF SYMBOLS AND SACRED OBJECTS*

"The spiral was concocted with the idea of death and rebirth: entering the mysterious earth womb, penetrating to its core, and passing out again by the same route."

—BARBARA G. WALKER

"The music flows within me like pure spirit. What a wonderful conversation within the flow of universal energy!"

—A MODERN PRAYER FROM VIENNA, AUSTRIA, FROM *THE BRIDGE OF STARS,* EDITED BY MARCUS BRAYBROOKE

Consulting the Spiral

Take the time to consider what your intention is before entering the spiral. What would you like to manifest in your life? What would you like help with? What would you like to get more direction and insight into? Here are a few questions that teenagers have taken into their spiral walk:

What is my next step in my life to be successful?

What is my path?

What do I need to do to prepare for leaving home?

How can I feel better about my choices?

How do I become stronger and more independent?

You can consult the spiral with concerns about relationships ("Give me insight into this relationship") or about any plan or idea ("Is this job a good idea for me?" "What is my next step with this project?"). Write down your request on a piece of paper and fold it up.

You may want to cleanse your energy before entering the spiral, to clear out any negativity. This can be done with a rattle, a feather, or the burning of sage. Cleansing negative energy with sage is called smudging in Native American traditions. Wave the rattle, the feather, or the smoldering sage around your body (or have someone else cleanse you this way). Know that your energy is being cleansed, so you may enter the spiral open and safe.

Now that your energy has been cleansed, enter the spiral through its threshold, bringing your written request with you. On the way into the center of the spiral, focus on your request. Walk slowly and mindfully until you reach the center. When your mind wanders off, just notice where your thoughts are and bring them back to your request and to walking the spiral.

Once you reach the center of the spiral, focus completely on your request. Take some time to fully *imagine* what your life will be like once your request has come true. What will happen? What will your relationships be like? Hold the feelings that you will have, imagine what your life will look like when this request becomes true for you. Place the request on the altar or under a stone. Leave it there with a small offering to the earth (seeds, a stone, a flower, tobacco) and thank spirit for hearing and *answering* your request. Then begin to slowly walk back out of the spiral.

As you circle out of the spiral, your request is being answered. On your return walk, notice what thoughts, experiences, animals, sounds, and smells get your attention. As you enjoy the walk out, pay attention to what crosses your path (internally and externally). Know that your request has been heard. When you pass through the threshold again, acknowledge that you are leaving the sacred space and entering back into the world of the mundane.

Continue to pay attention to what crosses your path for two weeks. Spirit has been sent a request and you will be getting responses. Watch for that surprise package in the mail!

Justin, age nineteen, experienced a change of heart as a result of his spiral walk:

"I have always been afraid because my dad has always been afraid. He always has excuses about why a job hasn't worked for him, and he is never happy. I wanted to be free of my father's negativity. As I walked into the spiral, I kept asking for help to release my dad's negativity. Then in the center I took the time to see what my life could be if I wasn't like my dad. It's weird but it just struck me then that I am not my dad. Just walking a spiral proves that. We are two different people. I love my dad but I don't want to be my dad. I felt I left my dad in the center of the spiral and came out with more of myself. It is hard to explain to others but I am braver now."

Your walk through the spiral has awakened your shakti. Sometimes waking up the shakti gets us feeling impatient to express ourselves. Notice how you choose to express your shakti. Are you tempted to fall back into negative habits or are you really opening yourself to something new?

Neale, who is eighteen, asked if it would be a good time to move in with his girlfriend. He had mixed feelings and wanted to consult the pendulum. He had a sense that he had an answer within himself but couldn't get to it by going over it in his mind.

Consulting The Pendulum

The answer Neale received from the pendulum was yes—this would be a good time to move in with his girlfriend. Interestingly, he decided to move out of state to attend college and the couple are postponing their plans to live together. Here is what Neale says about consulting the pendulum:

"If you can't 'see' it, you can't create it."

—COLLEEN BRENZY, INTUITIVE HEALER, PHILOSOPHER

"If you are a dreamer, come in
If you are a dreamer, a wisher, a liar,
A hope-er, a pray-er, a magic bean buyer . . .
If you're a pretender, come sit by my fire
For we have some flax-golden tales to spin.
Come in!
Come in!"

—SHEL SILVERSTEIN, AUTHOR OF
WHERE THE SIDEWALK ENDS

A Simple Yes or No Will Do: Consulting the Pendulum

Sometimes, your shakti will bring up an idea that involves making what seems like a big decision. Instead of being inspired and energized, you may find yourself feeling indecisive and frustrated. A pendulum can help you break this stalemate, by giving you a quick yes-or-no response. This technique uses your energetic Rainbow Body to help you move more quickly toward finding an answer to your question.

A pendulum can be a favorite necklace or a crystal or quartz at the end of a chain or string. You can use anything that you value that can swing easily from your hand when you hold it out. Barbara Brennan, in her book *Hands of Light,* recommends using pear-shaped pendulums made of beechwood. Mine is a favorite necklace made of turquoise and red coral.

Make sure that the pendulum is infused with your energy if it is newly purchased. You can do this by placing the pendulum in your left hand and imagining a gauge that reads FULL, then slowly goes down to EMPTY. This represents emptying out other people's energy from the pendulum. Then place the pendulum in your right hand and imagine the gauge going from empty to full. You are filling the pendulum with your energy.

Give yourself about five minutes to do the exercise, and a few more minutes to journal.

Hold the pendulum about six inches away from your body. Still the pendulum completely. Then ask the pendulum to show you a yes response. In a few moments it will begin to swing front to back or left to right. Notice which way it swings and note that this is your yes response. The other direction is then your no response. Still the pendulum once more and bring your question into mind. You need to formulate the question in a yes-or-no fashion.

Ask your question out loud. Then watch to see which way the pendulum swings. Trust whatever answer comes. Whether or not you follow its advice is still your choice. Consider keeping your questions and responses in your psychic journal, so you can remember your question, the response you got, and what you did about it.

"I find myself consulting it whenever I need some clarity. I don't always follow it but it eases my mind because I can stop thinking about the issue. It felt great to know that it would be okay to move in with my girlfriend—knowing this ended up freeing me to make other choices. Strange, but we are both happy about my decision to go away to college."

Letting Go Is Getting

Try this simple visualization technique for manifesting your desires and goals. It helps you get a better sense of exactly what it is you want. Take a moment to ground and rest in your breath . . .

Imagine—see in your mind—your goal or desire. Focus all your energy into really seeing it. Continue to breathe, and relax into the image . . . Put as much detail into this image as you can. Take out things that don't feel right and add things that do.

Now infuse this image with your desire and enthusiasm to have it become real for you. Imagine sending into it all your positive energy and excitement. Feel your body engage in this infusion . . . empowering this image as much as possible.

Repeat the above steps three times, noticing how you improve on your image each time you re-create it. You can even journal about this exercise after you re-create the image the third time and come back to it later to refine and re-create it one final time.

Now it is time to let this image go . . . see it being released, like letting go of a kite string, see it floating away, up into the sky, and disappearing out of sight. You are sending out this image, empowered and infused with your energy and love, to meet up with the creative power that is out there.

"Look. This is your world! You can't not look. There is no other world. This is your world: it is your feast. You inherited this: you inherited these eyeballs; you inherited this world of color. Look at the greatness of the whole thing. Look! Don't hesitate—look! Open your eyes. Don't blink, and look, look—look further."

—CHÖGYAM TRUNGPA, TIBETAN LAMA, AUTHOR OF *SHAMBHALA: THE SACRED PATH OF THE WARRIOR*

YOUR PERSONAL TIMING: GETTING IN SYNC

All through school you have been expected to function according to other people's timing. You have to show up for class at scheduled times and make sure to get your assignments in at a required time. There seems to be a "right" time for everything—when you should start dating, when you should attend college, when you should get a "real" job, when you should get married. Although there is a *natural* timing for everything in nature, human beings have lost touch with this natural timing. Our culture really interferes with our own natural and personal rhythms—advertisements, popular television shows and movies, music, social organizations, and businesses all dictate what you should be doing, and when.

Spiritual teachers and shamans realize that each of us has his or her own natural rhythms, his or her own pace. Like fingerprints, each person's timing is unique.

> *"I am an honor student and do well in all my classes. I tend to wait to the last minute and cram for tests. This drives my mother and father nuts because they are planners and have a completely different way of doing things. They also are very worried that I will give up school to get married. That's because my mother felt forced to get married before she finished with college and now regrets it. I have no intention of getting married soon. And so far, this cramming has worked okay for me."*
>
> —JESSICA, AGE 18

Not surprisingly, many people suffer because they are caught between what *feel*s like the appropriate time to do something and when others expect them to do it. Some people live their entire lives according to timetables imposed by other people. If you know any

"People have a tendency to move either too fast or too slow. They are tuned into what others are saying about them and forgetting to get in touch with their own internal clock."

—COLLEEN BRENZY, INTUITIVE HEALER, PHILOSOPHER

"Let us not look back in anger or forward in fear, but around in awareness."

—JAMES THURBER, AMERICAN WRITER, HUMORIST, CARTOONIST

unhappy adults, you will probably discover that they have been denying their own sense of timing. An example might be: "My grandfather wanted my dad to put off school and stay and help him on the farm, so he never did make it to college."

Feeling out of sync with what society sees as the "ideal" timetable and pace for life can distort your self-image. Back in 1991 I was feeling upset with myself. All my life I had felt I was lazy. I liked those times I gave myself to just hang out at home, reading or doing nothing. But I always had some unfinished project hanging over my head. I often felt overwhelmed by the feeling that I was a lazy person. Now it was so much on my mind that I shared it with my spiritual adviser.

She smiled at me and asked, "How many books have you written so far? Isn't it true you have a successful business and own your own home, and you find time to play and relax?" I laughed at myself. She had a point. If I was so *lazy,* how had I written three books and managed to have a full work and personal life, with time left over to just relax? I discovered that I was beating myself over the head with other people's notions of timing. My timing included hanging-out time, and that to just relax and do nothing is not necessarily being lazy. I had thought my life should "look" a certain way but it wasn't *my* way.

To manifest your own personal goals and dreams, you need to honor your own timing. Your energy body will have its own unique rhythm and pace. Tuning in to your own timing will help alleviate frustration at not doing things when other people are doing them, and will empower you to make choices based on when the time is right *for you.* Nothing cramps your creative spirit like feeling pressured to do something when you aren't ready or being prevented from doing something when you do feel ready.

There is no grand rule book in the sky that says you have to get your driver's license as soon as you reach the legal age, or get married before a certain age, that college has to take exactly four years

"... I am circling around God, around the ancient tower,
and I have been circling for a thousand years,
and I still don't know if I am a falcon, or a storm, or a great song."
—RAINER MARIA RILKE, GERMAN POET

and then you have to go into graduate school right away. *You can choose.* You can tune in to your own pace, and your own sense of timeliness, of readiness. All the exercises in this book will help you get in sync with your own timing.

When You Feel Impatient

When you feel frustrated and impatient about your goals, try this: Slow down and take some quiet time to answer the following questions in your journal.

1. State what it is that you feel you are not accomplishing. For example: "I am not a millionaire." "I may not get into that college that offers journalism." "That girl I really like may not want to go out with me."

2. Ask yourself, *Is my goal realistic?* Give yourself some time with this question. If your goal is to be a millionaire in one year, does that sound realistic? Is getting into that particular college realistic, given your grades and other admissions criteria? Are this girl's interests and personality traits really compatible with your own? Consider this question and be as honest as you can.

3. *Do I know the steps I need to take to get to my goal?* Write out all the steps you would need to follow to get to your goal. For example:

    - Call the school for an application
    - Complete and send the application to the school
    - Check out financial aid
    - Ask parents for financial support

Holding a goal over your head can be quite frightening and make it very difficult to take the next step. So, take one step at a time. This really does make it easier. Once you have decided that your goal is

> "People, like plants and trees, grow according to their own inner clock as well as in relationship to the outer seasons. It is important to respect the rhythms and seasons in each of our lives and to pay attention to dreams and synchronistic events that will help us to grow in an organic way."
>
> —JEAN SHINODA BOLEN, M.D., AUTHOR OF *THE TAO OF PSYCHOLOGY*

realistic, what is the *next* step that will move you toward it? And the next? Hold the goal in your heart like a horizon to move toward and see the steps as the road that will lead you there.

To manifest means to make something real. When you create, when you manifest something, you are expressing the divine; or the divine is expressing itself through you. In fact, the divine seeks to create through us. Everything, alive or not, even a rock, as still as it may be, is an expression of the divine. So when you take yourself out into the world and begin to express yourself, you are showing that you and the divine are one.

Your creative act doesn't have to be a big deal. You may be at your most creative in your simplest moments. Reading a poem to a child, talking to a stranger at the bus stop, sending a letter to a friend, all are simple but valuable acts. Then there will be times when the result of your creative impulse will be a bigger deal—inventing something, writing a book, speaking up, painting a picture, starting a business, or getting an article in the paper. Big deal or small, what matters is that you keep that creative energy always moving through you.

Across the wall of the world,
A River sings a beautiful song. It says,
Come, rest here by my side.

• • •

Lift up your eyes
Upon this day breaking for you.
Give birth again
To the dream.

—MAYA ANGELOU, FROM
ON THE PULSE OF MORNING

"Ojibwe women weave a net in a willow hoop, just like grandmother Spider's, and hang it over the crib of their babies. It's a reminder of the gift of a Grandmother, and a reminder that most gifts come from places where we least expect them."
—DENNIS L. OLSON, AUTHOR OF SHARED SPIRITS

"They are sending a voice to me.
From the place where the sun goes down,
Our Grandfather is sending a voice to me.
From where the sun goes down,
They are talking to me as they come.
Our Grandfather's voice is calling to me.
That winged One there where the Giant lives,
Is sending a voice to me. He is calling me.
Our Grandfather is calling me!"

—OGLALA SIOUX ELDER,
CHANTING FOR A VISION

7
The Path of the Visionary
Activating Your Psychic Vision

⊚ SCOTT'S VISION QUEST DREAM ⊚

Scott went on a vision quest with four other high school seniors, who would all be graduating in another few weeks. After fasting for the day to help prepare them to receive a personal vision, they participated in a Calling of a Vision Ceremony (see The Thundering Years: Rituals and Sacred Wisdom for Teens*). The five then went off to find a place to sleep under the stars alone for the night. Scott set out to climb a steep hill with a friend who was an athlete. He wanted to go as high and as far as she did. But when he was about halfway up he found a place that called to him. It was a little inlet, in the shape of a half moon, tucked into the hillside. Above him, to the east, a half moon was rising, while behind him in the west the sun began to set.*

His friend trekked farther up the hill. Scott heard her footsteps fade. He rolled out his sleeping bag, then sat on the grass and watched as the sun went down and the darkness surrounded him. He felt the power in the

"I have searched in the darkness, being silent in the great lonely stillness of the dark. So I became an *angakoq*,* through visions and dreams and encounters with flying spirits."

—NAJAGNEG, AN INUIT SHAMAN, TRANSLATED BY JOAN HALIFAX, *SHAMANIC VOICES*

*An angakoq is an owl.

"Trust in yourself. Your perceptions are often far more accurate than you are willing to believe."

—CLAUDIA BLACK, AUTHOR OF *CHANGING COURSE: HEALING FROM LOSS, ABANDONMENT, AND FEAR*

"Adepts of all religions speak of experiencing or seeing light around people's heads."

—BARBARA ANN BRENNAN, AUTHOR OF *HANDS OF LIGHT*

place he had chosen, its shape mimicking the rising moon, and he trusted that spirit was already working with him. He remembered the story of Half-boy that had been told during the Calling of a Vision ceremony. He sat quietly, a half boy waiting for a vision that might make him whole.

Soon he fell asleep and slept beautifully and soundly, like he had never slept before, until a rustling sound awakened him in the dark. The sound brought up some fear: What could be making so much noise? he thought. Was he in danger? After waiting tensely for a few moments he saw a rabbit emerge from the darkness and approach him. He relaxed, amazed at how something so small could bring up such fear. Then he fell asleep again and dreamt.

He dreamed he visited the other four questers. They gathered around the fire together until horrible creatures from beyond appeared, with the intention to destroy them all. He fought a bloody and fearsome battle but he conquered them all and everyone was safe.

He awoke to see the moon passing behind him, and although he could see only half of it, he felt its fullness. He was not afraid. Now he felt his own fullness. He had a deeper sense of who he was. He felt his courage, and knew he could draw on it whenever he became afraid. He knew he could succeed at following his dreams. He also sensed the fullness of his fellow questers. He knew the potential and promise that were inherent in each one of them. He could feel all this inside of him as he lay in the dark, alone.

At the fire where the questers gathered the next morning, everyone shared the stories and visions they had had. The leaders acted as mirrors, retelling the young people's journeys back to each of them to further validate their experience. Scott also mirrored back to the circle how their stories spoke of the truth about them. He mirrored their beauty and their strengths, just as a shaman would. It was obvious to everyone in the group that Scott had shamanic vision.

No one knows how Scott will express this shaman self as he leaves home. What does seem clear is that his life will be different now that spirit has made contact with him and he has heard its call.

 THE SHAMAN'S CELESTIAL JOURNEY

This myth tells the story of the Carib shamans of Suriname, in South America.

I say goodbye to my mother and father, my brothers and my sisters and all the friends of my youth, for I am going on a journey from which I will not return as the one who set off.

Six of us are chosen. I wonder if the others are as proud and as afraid as I. For twenty-four days and twenty-four nights we will be in training for the journey, isolated from the village, living with our Master in a hut set aside in the forest, covered with palm leaves. By day we will work hard, tending to the Master's tobacco fields, felling a sacred tree and carving the important alligator bench from its wood, whittling our magic staffs, and shaping the bells we will use if and when we are initiated as shamans. By night we will be instructed on how to make the journey.

Six days and six nights pass. For three of these we have worked and fasted, and for three we have rested. The alligator bench is ready, but so far none of us has watched for a vision on it. At night, after we have danced and sung until we are exhausted, we sit on it listening to the Master's instruction. He is teaching us about the spirit world. If we cannot have conversations with spirits we cannot be shamans. We must know their names, their natures, the locations where they may be found, the ways they can help us, and the ways they can hinder us. We are taught about the great Grandfather Spirit, the Creator, but we will never see him or speak with him directly. Grandfather Vulture speaks for the great Grandfather Spirit.

Six more days and nights go by. We smoke, we chew tobacco leaves, we drink tobacco juice. We are instructed in everything about the animal kingdom. My hunger is tearing at my body. I cannot endure it. I crouch. I stalk

**"Be careful on the journey, they said,
The journey to heaven.
They warned me.
And so I went.**

. . .

Visions are everywhere."

—KASHIA POMO, TRANSLATED BY GEORGE QUASHA

my prey. I leap. I tear flesh. I am jaguar—and blood runs from my jaws.

I remember . . . What do I remember? I search . . . but cannot find my name.

What time has passed? I do not know. Much time is spent lying on the alligator bench waiting for visions. If they do not come, I will not be a shaman. What do I see? Movements in the shadows. They are here—the spirits—but they will not speak to me.

The Master stretches ropes taut across the hut at different levels. First we dance on the low ones. Then we go higher and higher. I am above the world. I hang from the ropes by my fingers. I see the world dissolving and, standing before me in the air, a benevolent spirit. I cry out to him but he is already gone. I have had no conversation. Will I fail? Will I fail! My stomach is empty. My eyes are wild. There is roaring in my ears. I dance. I dance . . . Suddenly he is before me, naked and ancient, Grandfather Vulture himself, showing me the spiral ladder my Master has told me about.

"Come," he says, "come. It is time for your journey."

I step onto the ladder. It feels like air, but holds me firm. I step. I step. I turn. I am climbing to the sky. I am journeying to the sky. I come upon a village. Everyone in it is white as smoke. They ignore me. Beside a river I meet a beautiful woman who draws me into the water. I swim with her and, as we move together like one being, she teaches me spells. When I leave the water Grandfather Vulture leads me to the crossroads of Life and Death. There I must choose to go to the Land Without Evening or to the Land Without Dawn. As I approach one, the light dazzles me. As I approach the other, the darkness blinds me.

Suddenly a searing pain shoots through my body and I find myself in the hut again, the Master bending over me and ants biting me.

"You must not go too far, too fast," the Master says. "It is not time to know these things yet."

"Everything in our lives can wake us up or put us to sleep, and basically it's up to us to let it wake us up."

—PEMA CHÖDRÖN, *START WHERE YOU ARE*

More time passes. I do not know how much. I am beyond hunger and thirst.

The Master puts me on a platform suspended from the ceiling of the hut and releases the cords he had twisted to hold it steady. It swings around and around. As I revolve I pass through the many celestial spheres of the universe. I see darkness and light run together like one thing and in that one thing I see the spirits dance. They speak to me. They cry out. Some enter my body and I scream and shake with the pain—wishing my Master would drive them out. I am torn apart. I lie bleeding. The spirits leave me and I am empty, like a nutshell abandoned on the floor of the forest. But others come to me and lead me on and up. They fill me with their wisdom. I am full. I am whole. I can speak with spirits. I am a shaman!

—ADAPTED BY JULIE TALLARD JOHNSON FROM *MYTHICAL JOURNEYS/LEGENDARY QUESTS*, BY MOYRA CALDECOTT

BRINGING ON THE VISIONS

Visions are messages from the world of spirit that come to you through your dreams, encounters with the natural world, synchronicities (meaningful coincidences), and *journeying*—where you intentionally communicate with the spiritual world. When making contact with the spiritual world, you are contacting both the higher self within you and an external, greater power that is available to us all. Spirit speaks to us in many ways, every day. This chapter is about opening up and listening for its call.

The ancients taught their teens to listen to and trust their visions. These visions came in day *and* night dreams. Black Elk, Jesus, Padmasambhava, past and present Dalai Lamas, and Jackie Yellow Tail (Crow medicine woman) all trusted their visions to guide them on their chosen paths.

> "Every time you don't follow your inner guidance, you feel a loss of energy, loss of power, a sense of spiritual deadness."
>
> —SHAKTI GAWAIN, AUTHOR OF *DEVELOPING INTUITION*

You don't need to be a recognized shaman to have visions. In fact, each of us has access to personal visions. There are many ways to call a vision to you—in shamanic traditions you do it by journeying. In the above stories, the traveler did not go far *physically* from his village or home, but traveled far psychically and had extraordinary, insightful encounters with spirits. Some would describe these experiences as "only a dream," or say that the boy in the second story was hallucinating. Others will say that both young men have journeyed and walked with the spirit world. What do you believe? Have you had a dream that felt very real and meaningful? Have you gone on a vision quest or shamanic journey?

This chapter is about intentionally taking such journeys. As both of the preceding stories demonstrate, it is best to take these journeys with a skilled teacher or to have done some preparatory work. If you have practiced many of the exercises in this book, you are ready to open up to some personal visions. You too may discover that you are a shaman. At the very least you will discover your visionary self, your psychic self—the self that connects you to the all the shamans past, present, and future.

Journeying is a form of *creative visualization*. Being able to visualize (see images in your mind) is a basic tool needed for journeying. Many of us have difficulty "seeing" images in our minds. The following is a simple meditation that helps you develop this valuable skill.

GOLD DOT MEDITATION

This Zen meditation practice will help you focus your attention during journeying and visualizations. It is a very simple meditation that will help you "see" things when you journey.

Close your eyes. Visualize one and a half feet in front of your face a gold dot. Breathe and relax, while maintaining your attention on this gold dot. Do this meditation for three to five minutes.

This exercise brings your attention to the present moment and can also help bring focus to other areas of your life, such as exams and complex reading material. The more you practice the creative visualization exercises in this book, the more you will develop your visualizing skills.

THE PATH OF THE SHAMAN

Shamanic journeying is similar in some ways to the creative visualizations you have been doing throughout this book. There are important differences, as José and Lena Stevens point out in *Secrets of Shamanism*: "Unlike planned visualizations, in the shamanic journey process you don't always know what is going to happen in your visions. You don't control the events and situations that you experience but you can control how you respond to them." Journeying, then, is much like dreaming—you can't often control the dream but you can decide how you want to respond to the dream.

In the stories that opened this chapter, both young men were *journeying*. When you journey you will be opening the door between yourself and the spirit world—something we all did quite naturally as children. You will find that in shamanic journeying the most important and powerful tool is, once again, your *imagination*.

"A shaman is a man or woman who enters an altered state of consciousness—at will— to contact and utilize an ordinarily hidden reality in order to acquire knowledge, power, and to help other persons. The shaman has at least one, and usually more, 'spirits' in his personal service."

—FROM MICHAEL HARNER'S *THE WAY OF THE SHAMAN*

Because in your teenage years you are in closer touch with your imagination, you will not find it difficult to have a "shamanic vision." For you it may be a matter of *trusting* that what you experience is truly a vision.

"I attended a shamanic drumming circle with my mother one night. She really wanted me to have this experience, so I decided I would give it a try. Each night the leader chooses a topic to guide the journey. That night the leader said that we would be journeying to ask for a vision about any fears we might have. This was perfect for me because I was really afraid of being alone. It is even hard for me to describe, but the thought of being alone just freaks me out. So that is the fear I picked.

"The leader began to drum and drum and guided us on a shamanic journey. We visualized entering a hole in the ground where we would go into the underworld for help. It was easy for me. And the thing is, it felt real. I know I was experiencing all this in my head, yet it was more than that.

"I found a creature that was holding my fear, like a weapon it used against me. Then I called for some animal to help me release the fear. Crow showed up and took my fear from this creature and flew it into a river. The river was moving very fast and the fear just disappeared under the currents. The crow came back to me, gave me one of its feathers, and told me that I can call on him any time I need him."

—MICHELE, AGE 18

Journeying can be simple or complex. You can journey to receive a vision, as in the preceding stories. You can journey to connect with your power animal. You can journey to heal parts of your psyche and

"The challenge of adolescence, as in all the stages of growth, is to find the self and remain true to the self through all the chaos of physical and emotional changes, sweet longings and painful rejections."
—BARBARA ANN BRENNAN, *HANDS OF LIGHT*

body, or to get an answer to a question. You can use journeying to get what you need to create your life.

All the practices that follow are presented in a way that allows you to do them on your own. Consider me your guide.

A Shamanic Journey

Drumming is traditionally used by shamans to help guide the journey. There are many shamanic drumming CDs available that have preset timings for your journeying. It is best to start out with a brief journey of about five to fifteen minutes the first couple of times. Some CDs have voices guiding you through a journey, while others just offer simple instruction and drumming.

Begin your journey in a place where you know you are safe, giving yourself enough time to have a complete journey without being disturbed. Formulate your question. What is it that you want this journey to be about? The following questions are examples of how to focus your journey.

What is the next step I need to take in my life?

How can I be less afraid of . . . ?

How can I get stronger about . . . ?

Would so-and-so make a good friend?

What should I do after I graduate from high school?

How can I resolve the problem I have with . . . ?

Now lie down on the floor in a comfortable position. Close your eyes and take a couple of deep breaths, letting your body relax into the floor as you exhale. Feel the heaviness of your body on the floor, giving it permission to relax down into the floor.

"I build a home between Earth and Spirit, I work from the creative ground of my Soul. I nourish the World with the Soul's Rainbow Light."

—AFFIRMATION FOR THE FLOWER ESSENCE OF IRIS, FROM *AFFIRMATIONS*, THE FLOWER ESSENCE SOCIETY

"Dreams have always been an important part of my life. I think that is true for most people who are searching for spirituality and go out and fast. Dreams guide you; they show you the way that you should be living, or the direction, or give you signs to help someone else, and they are gifts."

—JACKIE YELLOW TAIL, CROW WOMAN, FROM *WALKING IN THE SACRED MANNER*

"Wait until you are calm and relaxed before undertaking this or any other shamanic exercise. Avoid psychedelic or alcoholic substances during the preceding twenty-fours, so that your centeredness and power of concentration will be good, and your mind clear of confusing imagery."

—FROM MICHAEL HARNER'S *THE WAY OF THE SHAMAN*

Imagine yourself lying on the ground in some natural place outdoors. In this place there is a cave entrance nearby, or some opening into the earth. This opening can be a place you have actually visited if one comes to mind. Bring this place into focus and rest your full attention on this image of the cave entrance. This opening goes down deep into the earth, where there are many caverns and rooms. The opening should feel both familiar and comfortable for you.

Start the drumming CD. Slowly approach the entrance to the cave and enter the opening. Notice the smells of the rich earth, the stillness of the tunnel, the feel of your body as it enters this place. Just inside the entrance of the cave, you will meet a spirit guardian that will help you on your journey. It may come in the form of an animal, a guardian angel, an ancestor, a ball of energy, a person, or a voice. This being will be your spirit guide on your shamanic journey.

Tell your guide your question. Your guide then will lead you down a tunnel into the underworld. This passage is usually short, ending in a room or a place in nature. Your guide has taken you to a place where you will encounter the animals, beings, voices, or symbols you need to answer your question. Trust whatever comes. You may get a simple "Yes, go ahead . . ." or "You'd better be careful . . ." or you may be taken on a dreamlike journey. Just go with the experience and keep focused on the journey. Let the drumming keep you focused. You want to be present for whatever happens on the journey.

When either the drumming becomes rapid, thus calling you back to the room, or you are told in your vision that the journey is done, bring yourself back to the place where you entered the underworld. Thank your guide and come back through the tunnel and out of the cave opening. Don't bring anything back with you from your journey that you didn't take in with you.

Then feel yourself in your body and back in the room, on the floor, breathing. Take some time to reacquaint yourself with the room. When you feel ready, take the time to journal your experience.

It may take a few attempts before you get a strong sense that you have journeyed. Be patient and practice several times. By the third time, you will likely have a very meaningful journey and vision.

If you are interested in longer and more in-depth journeying, I recommend you refer to the Shamanism resources listed at the end

The Basics of Shamanic Journeying

1. Give yourself some sacred time and space where you will be safe and undisturbed for the needed amount of time.
2. Have a shamanic drumming CD and a CD player ready or a shamanic healer drumming and guiding your journey.
3. Lie comfortably on the floor, breathing deeply.
4. Focus on your question.
5. Travel to the "underworld," which represents going within.
6. Meet your spirit guardian.
7. Tell your guardian your question.
8. Travel down the tunnel.
9. Arrive in a room.
10. Receive your journey vision.
11. Return and reflect on your experience.

of the book. You can also go to www.shamanism.com or e-mail shaman@shamanism.com to find the shamanic drumming circle nearest you.

Interpreting Shamanic Journeys

You will relate to your journey much as you would interpret a dream. The images and actions in your dreams have very personal and unique meanings for you, and it is the same with the visions you will have on a journey. You are the best person to interpret your journey, although you may want to share it with a trusted friend or elder or a shamanic practitioner. Take the time to record your journey. By drawing it or writing it in your journal, you can get more insight into its meaning for you. Most times, the vision you experience is very simple and obvious and leaves little need for interpretation. Shamanic practitioners may have additional insights due to their experience, but your own understanding of the journey should be the principal one. Trust your own understanding of the journey.

DREAM VISIONS

In many traditions, journeying is really "dreaming" during the day. In fact, your dreams can also hold visions.

Ihan'bla is the Plains Indian term for dreams. Dreams are considered by the Plains Indians to be a direct communication with the spirit world. Ihan'bla dreams can come while you are awake or asleep. In Tibetan dream yoga, dreams are considered a means of accessing one's true nature. To listen to your dreams, then, means to be listening to the spirit world and to your own inner guide.

Your nighttime dreams can help you live the dreams you hold in

"Pearls do not lie on the seashore. If you desire one, you must dive for it."
—CHINESE PROVERB

"An unexamined dream is like an unopened letter."
—THE TALMUD,
JEWISH HOLY TEXT

your heart during the day. They may be encouraging you to follow your dreams even when someone, perhaps a parent or even a coach, is pushing you in a different direction.

"My mother was this way with me. Emotionally she was an unsympathetic person, who never much wanted to talk about stuff of a personal nature. For most of my teen years, however, we considered ourselves 'friends,' meaning mostly that she would confide in me about how unhappy she was with my father. But she could never handle my stories, my personal journeys. So I stopped trying to tell her much of anything. Slowly I began to accept that I was not the daughter she wanted. She wanted an extension of herself, someone to play with, to drink with, and to attend sporting events with. I was never this girl, although at times I would try to be who she wanted me to be. I often felt as if I had her face on me—and underneath it was my true face, hidden.

"At the age of seventeen, I had this dream. My mother had come home with a lot of groceries. She was carrying them in. I was in the back of the house where there was an indoor sauna. I was in the sauna, when my brother walked in and began to push me against the hot sauna rocks. My skin was burning. Then he stabbed me with a knife. I went out into the kitchen where my mother was putting groceries away and cried out loud to her. I was standing there bleeding with a knife stuck in my stomach. She just walked right by me and kept putting groceries away."

—ANNETTE, AGE 24

> **"Jesus said, 'Show me the stone which the builders have rejected. That one is the cornerstone.'"**
> —THE GOSPEL OF THOMAS

With this dream Annette began to realize that she felt invisible to her mother, and that it would be up to her to keep herself safe and happy.

Remember the eagle who thought he was a chicken? Annette's mother didn't see her daughter's true nature. But Annette wasn't going to die a chicken!

At the age of twenty-three, Annette had another dream:

"I dreamt I was married to my mom. Twice young men were interested in me and then they found out I was married to my mother. They weren't objecting to her being my mother as much as the age difference. She was lying on the sofa. Two men came into the room. One whispered, 'Is she married?' pointing at me. The other one said, 'Yes, to her,' pointing to my mother.

"I then got up and went into my bedroom and looked into the mirror. I told myself I couldn't stay married to my mother. I thought that if I knew someone who was married to their mom it would be strange. I decided to tell my mom I wanted a divorce. I went out and she was sitting at a table with a glass and some wine in a bottle. She had a sense of what I was going to tell her. She poured the wine into the glass and it spilled over. I told her it would be better if she didn't drink. I also told her that I was not going to drink with her anymore. Then I walked out of her house on my own.

"In my day life, I did stop drinking with her. As a result my relationship with her changed dramatically. These dreams guided me to protect myself when it came to my mother. They helped me become whole. They were personal dreams that held a message, a vision for me. I believe we all have such dreams, such messages that are attempting to help us and guide us."

Tibetan Dream Yoga

Tibetans practice an elaborate (but not difficult) process of dream yoga that allows you to use your dreams to become more present

"At the heart of all religions is the certainty that there is a fundamental truth, and that life is a sacred opportunity to evolve and realize it."

—SOGYAL RINPOCHE,
TIBETAN LAMA

and happy in your life. It is an ancient process that teaches you to "awaken" in your dreams and to be able to receive the visions that appear in your dream time. You can tune in more clearly to the visions in your dreams by following the suggestions below, which are based on the Tibetan model:

- Record your dreams in your psychic journal. This can be done by drawing your dreams or by writing them out.
- Listen to your dreams and respond to them, as Annette did in the above example. She let her dreams play an important role in guiding her decisions, and ultimately the course of her life. Consider your dreams letters or messages from your true nature or the spirit world. What is being communicated to you?
- Before you go to sleep at night, ask for some guidance in your dream. Then to help you remember your dreams, traditional Tibetan practice instructs boys to lie on their right side and girls to lie on their left side.
- Share your dreams with trusted friends, your therapist, or your spiritual adviser.
- Notice what images, feelings, sensations, experiences, and encounters you had in your night dreams that also occur in the daytime.
- Read a good book on dreams for teens, such as *Teen Dream Power,* by M. J. Abadie.

Tibetan Dream Yoga, by Lama Surya Das (see the bibliography), is an excellent CD to take you more deeply into this journey.

"It can never be said too often that to realize the nature of mind is to realize the nature of all things."

—SOGYAL RINPOCHE, TIBETAN LAMA, AUTHOR OF *THE TIBETAN BOOK OF LIVING AND DYING*

MEETING YOUR POWER ANIMALS

In earlier days we understood that we are all part of the earth, and we held a deep respect for nature. We respected and honored spirits and thanked them for providing us with life, nourishment, and comfort. In these earlier times we gave recognition to the power of the animal spirits by wearing skins and masks, mimicking, singing praise, and sending prayers to specific animals. We painted the animals on our homes, clothes, faces, caves, and burial chambers. These acts allowed us to remain linked to the animal guides and to accept the power and lessons they offered us in life, and in death.

"The world is divided into various classes of animals, often referred to as the 'Two Leggeds,' 'Four Leggeds,' 'Wingeds,' and 'Those That Live in the Water.' Any of these, if acquired by a human as an ally, imparts powers peculiar to its kind."

—MARK ST. PIERRE AND TILDA LONG SOLDIER,
AUTHORS OF *WALKING IN THE SACRED MANNER*

"You're a fine young man
You Grizzly Bear
You crawl out of your fur
You come
I say Whu Whu Whu!
I throw grease in the fire
For you
Grizzly Bear
We're one!"

—TLINGIT INVOCATION,
VERSION BY DAVID CLOUTIER

Each animal has powerful spirits, medicine, and inherent skills. Power animals, also called animal totems, come to you in your dreams or in physical form because they have a lesson you need to learn or a "power" they are willing to share with you. They seek to give you a gift of understanding, of love, energy, and knowledge.

Animal spirits choose a person to be a companion to, a friend to, not the other way around. They choose you, as the red-tailed hawk chose me and as the black panther chose Hailey (see story on page 201). Your power animals will choose you by coming to you in your dreams or in your journeying and making themselves known to you. You will only need to pay attention to discover who your power animals are. Once you come to know which animals are your power animals, you can go on journeys to ask them for help and guidance.

Hailey went on a vision quest and encountered her power animal—the black panther. While she slept under the stars, she felt the breath of some animal on her face and dreamt of the black panther. One of the shamanic guides who led the vision quest awoke that same night and felt that Hailey was being "visited" by the black panther. She woke the other leader and asked if black panthers were found in this area. (They are rare, but do visit this area.) They both sent out protective energy to Hailey and could sense that she was safe.

In the circle the next morning Hailey and the guides shared their experiences, and everyone agreed that Hailey had been visited by the panther. The panther then became her power animal. The medicine of this animal resonated with Hailey's view of herself and her life. Its power includes a silent dignity, independence, and courage in difficult times. It also gave her a place to focus and direct her energies. It became her guide and her totem. She would seek its guidance as one does with a higher power, and she carried the medicine of the black panther with her. She now wears a panther necklace around her neck and a tattoo of it on her foot.

Take the time to develop a relationship with your animal totem. Learn more about its physical characteristics, its habits, and its strengths, and think about how they relate to your life. Having an animal totem does not mean that you are to pet the animal or even be with it physically. Red-tail Hawk is a totem of mine, but I haven't touched one. Having an animal totem means that you have lessons to learn and a powerful spiritual friend. All totems are powerful but the meaning that the totem brings will vary depending on what type of animal has come to you.

"The unsaid for me exerts great power . . ."
—LOUISE GLÜCK, U.S. POET LAUREATE, WINNER OF PULITZER PRIZE

"Dive deep within:
You are bound to hear
The whispering
Peace-sea-messages."
—SRI CHINMOY, SPIRITUAL TEACHER

"The Creator gives us each a song."
—UTE SAYING

To meet your power animal, go on a shamanic journey as described previously. Focus your intention on acquiring a power animal to help you at this time in your life. When you greet the spirit guardian at the cave entrance, say that you are there to meet your power animal.

RUNNING PSYCHIC ENERGY

Psychic energy is your intuitive energy on full volume. You have this energy inside and around you. When you bring conscious awareness to this energy and use it skillfully, more of your true nature comes forth.

For thousands of years people who sought to be fully in touch with this energy have done so by going into a state of trance. "Going into trance" means to be one hundred percent in psychic space, to fully control your own psychic energy. It's like running a water faucet—the psychic energy is the water, your body is the faucet, and

Trancing enhances your psychic skills as well as your general well-being. Its benefits include:

- Opening up to your psychic energy
- Taking control of your own energy
- Stretching yourself to experience more states of consciousness
- Opening up to more of life's experiences
- Bringing balance to your Rainbow Body

your imagination is the hand that determines how much energy (water) flows. Being in a trance is like tuning into a TV station where the picture is clear and crisp. It is not about opening up to other spirits or other entities. In fact, when you run your own psychic energy, there is no room for other energies.

Taking the time to run your psychic energy will help bring balance into your life. If until now you have been closed off from your psychic energy, going into trance will help open it up for you. If you have been too open to this energy, trancing will help you filter it. During your teen years your psychic self is opening up—you are so much more sensitive to the energy around you and inside of you. This is an ideal time to begin the practice of going into trance.

The purpose of this practice is to focus your awareness and to stay present during the time that you are in trance. As you do when you are journeying, you want to remain alert. The Gold Dot meditation can help you build the focusing ability desired for this practice. I recommend practicing the Gold Dot meditation for a while before trying to go into trance.

Grounding yourself as part of the trancing is *vital*, because you will be running so much psychic energy. Too much psychic energy, without grounding, results in feeling out of control. It is like having the faucet running at full volume with no way of shutting it off. The grounding brings balance. Ideally, you have practiced the grounding meditation offered to you in chapter 1 for some time now. When you are properly grounded, trancing allows you to channel psychic energy correctly and creatively.

Going into Trance

When you are in trance, you will be using the same energy that you bring forth in meditation and journeying. You will want to run psychic energy with:

"We don't end at our skins."

—CHRISTIANE NORTHROP, M.D., HOLISTIC PHYSICIAN AND AUTHOR

"Answers that come through your intuitive processes or through channels may challenge what you would prefer to do. Your lower self, your personality, will not challenge, but rationalize."

—GARY ZUKAV, TAKEN FROM *THE SEAT OF THE SOUL*

"I believe that God is in me as the sun is in the color and fragrance of a flower—the Light in my darkness, the Voice in my silence."

—HELEN KELLER, BLIND AND DEAF AMERICAN EDUCATOR

- control
- breath
- intention
- focus

To begin, give yourself five minutes in a quiet place. Sit in a chair with your back erect, feet on the floor. Breathe and ground. Once you are grounded, bring down the psychic energy through your seventh chakra (the top of your head). Breathe and open up to this psychic energy from above. Pull it slowly down your spine to meet up with your grounding energy, blending the earth energy together with the psychic energy. From there your mixed energy will go down and out through the grounding cords into the earth. Breathe throughout this continuous energy exchange.

Now sit in this energy, aware and focused, for five minutes.

When it is time to break the trance, bend down and touch your palms to the floor.

Begin with five minutes of trancing a day. When you are in trance you need to *breathe.* Do not force things—do it with little effort. Make sure to pay attention while in trance, focus on running the energy. After you have practiced going into trance for a few weeks, you will be ready to do any of the exercises in this book again but now in trance.

Psychic energy can sometimes be like a jealous lover: It demands its time and wants to be exercised. I have learned this from my own experience. As I have explained earlier, as a teen I was continually aware of sharp insights into people and situations. This did not result in peace of mind or happiness but in a sensitivity that made it difficult

"Learn to get in touch with the silence within yourself and know that everything in this life has a purpose."
—ELISABETH KÜBLER-ROSS, AUTHOR OF *ON DEATH AND DYING*

Psychic Writing:
Communicating with Spirit

Psychic writing—going into a trance state while you write in your journal—is another practice that will help you to open up and communicate with spirit. This spirit can be a specific spiritual being, such as Christ, your guardian angel, or an ancestor. It can also be your own spirit, your true nature. As in journeying, it is important to trust what comes—breathe and go with the flow of the experience. Neale Donald Walsch's *Conversations with God for Teens* (see bibliography) has wonderful examples of psychic writing.

1. Begin by grounding and going into trance. Send out a prayer *intention*. What would you like to talk to God or spirit about? Request to hear the advice of a grandparent or ancestor in your family who has passed and whom you love and trust. Ask him or her to speak to you through your writing.
2. Write the question you have at the top of a page in your journal. For example:
   Dear Grandfather, please give me some advice on . . .
   Dear God/spirit, what do you think about . . .
   Dear guardian angel, what do you think I could do about . . .
3. Take a few deep breaths, and remember that you are in trance. Then write underneath your question:
   Dear (your name here),
   . . . and let the writing flow. Let your hand just move across the page as this spiritual connection takes place. Let your grandparent or spirit guide answer your question. Don't stop until you have written at least a paragraph's worth.
4. Thank the spirit for the guidance you have been given, and end the trance. Take some time to read over the message.

How will you know the message is really from spirit?
- It will *feel* true to you.
- It will somehow benefit everyone involved. There will be no harm suggested toward anyone. (Spirit doesn't take sides but understands everyone's perspective.)
- It will give you hope, insight, and courage.
- It will *sound* wise, like something that would come from a Wisdom Keeper—an ancestor or spirit.
- You feel the presence of a benevolent, loving being.

for me to relax and enjoy myself. Before I learned how to trance and direct my psychic energy, social gatherings weren't much fun for me. I would often find myself feeling stressed and overwhelmed at a party. I didn't completely understand that it was my psychic energy that had me "reading" and "seeing" into other people's psyches. It was my out-of-control psychic energy that was causing my stress. Finally, after taking the psychic development class and practicing the same meditations and exercises in this book—I can party! I can go into large groups and, having turned down the psychic volume, relax and enjoy myself. Going into trance on a regular basis makes my psychic self happy. Now I am in control of my psychic energy, and it no longer makes me feel out of control.

"The reverse also has a reverse side."

—JAPANESE PROVERB

"A genuine sense of humor is having a light touch. The basis of Shambhala vision is rediscovering that perfect and real sense of humor, that light touch of appreciation."

—CHÖGYAM TRUNGPA, TIBETAN MEDITATION MASTER AND TEACHER

LAUGH AND THE WORLD LAUGHS WITH YOU

Too many of our religious institutions try to scare people into following one specific doctrine, and often don't encourage you to think for yourself. That is why the Buddhists have a saying: "If you meet the Buddha on the street, kill him." In other words, after reading the Dharma (Buddhist teachings), put it down and go explore your own path. Don't make the teachings so central to your life that you lose sight of your own opinions and experience, or your sense of humor. Be *sincere* in your spiritual practices but not overly serious. A lack of fun and play means you are being too rigid. Being flexible will allow you to experience more in your life and in your journeying.

You can honor your psychic self without making too big a thing of it. Scott, the young man who experienced a vision on the hillside during a shamanic journey, can have that experience and then hang out with friends later that day. Don't take yourself too seriously. The fact is, when you can connect and laugh about the small and big stuff of life, it means you have relaxed enough to trust yourself, and spirit. So be playful with all the exercises. Let your pursuit be your play and your play be your pursuit. Experience these exercises and insights as pointers to the truth, not ironclad rules.

If the exercises in this book don't put a smile on your face and give you some hope and power, burn it. Use the book to make life better for you but then put the book down and go play—go live your life. Fortunately, teens don't usually have a hard time getting this point. Go explore your own path . . . it is a big, beautiful playground out there.

"I used to believe in reincarnation, but that was in a past life."
—PAUL KRASSNER,
INVESTIGATIVE SATIRIST

"Reality is the leading cause of stress amongst those in touch with it."
—JANE WAGNER, AUTHOR OF
THE SEARCH FOR SIGNS OF INTELLIGENT LIFE IN THE UNIVERSE

"I really feel sorry for people who think things like soap dishes or mirrors or Coke bottles are ugly, because they're surrounded by things like that all day long, and it must make them miserable."
—ROBERT RAUSCHENBERG,
AMERICAN PAINTER

"The temple bell stops
but the sound keeps coming
out of the flowers."

—BASHŌ, ZEN HAIKU MASTER

♡ 8
The Path with Heart
Emotional Wisdom

🌀 HAILEY'S STORY 🌀

I begin following my own path today. In just a matter of hours I will leave for a two-week hiking trip through the Grand Canyon and Colorado. I say two weeks, but I really have no idea how long it will be. And after that, I honestly do not know.

I have found that I like living my life that way. I leave myself open to the possibilities that lie before me. That's how I was able to make the decision to go to a college six hours away from the community in which I have lived my whole life.

When it was time to decide what my life would be like after high school, I had never had the experience of making a big life decision. A decision in which I was the sole decider, all that mattered was what I thought. First I thought I should take a year off from school, going to college later in my life. I was feeling terribly lost in the world and felt that I needed some time to figure myself out. Then a teacher told me to look at the University of Wisconsin-Superior as a possible college choice. He thought it would be a good fit. My rational thinking at the time was that I didn't want to live in northern Wisconsin. But I found myself checking out more about the college, and in my heart I felt that it was time to take a risk. I listened to my heart and applied for admission.

When I finally made a visit to the college, I knew this was where I wanted to be. As I walked around the campus I felt so happy and excited about coming there in the fall. I would meet new people and be able to reinvent myself.

I decided to follow this energy in my heart and see where it led me. My decision was a heavy one for my family. My parents were not ready to let their oldest daughter go out into the world. It brought a lot of stress into the relationship and they were not happy with my decision. But I had such a strong feeling that this was the next step for me, and I needed to follow that feeling wherever it led me, even if it was back home in a few months. I had no idea how things would turn out and that was part of the beauty inside myself. My heart would lead me, and my spirit and hard work would see me through. I knew this, and felt that everything would work out.

I can't say it has been easy for anyone, myself included, to leave everything I know behind. Yet, as I leave, I will begin to follow the path that will make me who I am. Every mistake I make along the way will be a mistake that I have to make, a thing to be learned from. Everything I have experienced has made me who I am, and I am forever changing. My parents eventually came to understand my decision. It doesn't make them happy, nor do they really agree with it. But our relationship will grow and change as I find who I am in the world and discover what I need to do.

So when I am asked that question "Why are you going all the way to Superior?" I give answers like "I want to play soccer for them" or "They have a good liberal arts program that will help me determine what I want to do." Which is all part of it. It is a beautiful place even when it is thirty below zero. But the truth is that I followed my self up there. There is no

"It makes no difference as to the name of the God, since love is the real God of all the world."
—APACHE SAYING

"Love one another and do not strive for another's undoing."
—SENECA INDIAN PROVERB

"rational decision" behind it. My path in life, which I was desperately try-ing to find, was inside me the entire time. I just needed to allow myself some spontaneity in making decisions, and to let my internal energy and desire for experience determine what I should be doing.

I am learning that it is not really necessary to explain oneself to any-one. Only you can make your decisions for you, and how you make them determines how happy you will be. My decisions will lead to growth, and nurture my experience. It not so much about "finding myself"—I am with myself all the time. It is about listening to myself, to my heart, and speak-ing from my heart. Everything else will somehow fall into place.

—HAILEY, AGE 18

🌀 ANCIENT STORY 🌀
by Dennis L. Olson

After Creator was done with most of creation he made two very special things. He called them Love and Honor, because they were made of most of the good feelings Creator had for the World. But he had one worry. It was the two-leggeds. He knew that they could take Love and Honor and twist them for selfish reasons. He knew they could make things seem like Love and Honor when they really weren't. He asked the animals for help.

At dawn, Eagle came soaring from the East. He offered to fly the spe-cial creation far up into the sky—eve to the Moon. "That will be a good hid-ing place," he told Creator.

The Creator thought about Eagle's offer for a while, but then shook his head.

"They will find them there," he said. "One day, another eagle will land on the Moon. It will have two-leggeds inside, and they will find the Special Gifts."

About noon, Mouse scurried to Creator from his home in the South.

> **"The prayer of the heart is the source of all good, refreshing the soul as if it were a garden."**
>
> —SAINT GREGORY OF SINAI, EGYPT

He offered to take the Gifts and bury them under the vast expanse of grasses on the prairie. "That will confuse them. The prairie is too big."

Creator thought this idea might work, but then he shook his head.

"No," he said. "Those two-leggeds will some day turn over the whole prairie with their iron plows. They will leave no room for the First People or the Buffalo. They will find the Gifts."

At sunset, Bear lurched to where Creator sat, huffing his way from his home in the West. He offered to take the Gifts to the high mountains and dig a deep cave. "If I put them there, the rocks will be too hard for the two-leggeds to dig, and they will give up."

Creator thought, and then shook his head again.

"Those two-leggeds are resourceful," he said. "One day they will take giant machines and dig the rock away. They will be looking for shiny things—things that will make them crazy. They will find the Gifts because they will dig holes in the Earth as big as the mountains."

When it was dark, the night cooled the air, and Wolf loped to where Creator sat. He came from his home in the far North. Wolf offered to take the Gifts to the farthest North spot. He could bury the Gifts in the huge sheet of ice and it would never melt. "They will never want to go there," he said.

Creator pondered Wolf's offer for a while, and then, sadly, shook his head again.

"I think those two-leggeds will have a curiosity which will make them do things just because they can," he said to Wolf. "They will not ask themselves if they should, because they will be so enamored with their skills, I think they will make special boats that will go under the Great Ice, and they will find the Gifts."

Creator sat until dawn, thinking. Just before the sun rose again, Mole pushed his strange fingered nose from the ground, between Creator's feet. Mole was startled at first, but then greeted Creator, and asked him what was troubling him. Creator explained the problem.

**"Every person,
All events of your life
Are there because you
    have drawn them
    there.
What you choose
To do with them is
Up to you."**

—RICHARD BACH,
AUTHOR OF *ILLUSIONS*

Mole was quiet for a while, but then spoke to Creator. "I know I am just a small Mole, and you are the Creator. I know you have asked the wisest animals in the Great Medicine Wheel to help you and they could not. I only know about the insides of the earth, the insides of things, but I have an idea. Why don't you take the Gifts of Love and Honor and bury them deep inside the hearts of these two-leggeds. They will never find them there . . ."

Creator did. And you know, to this day, the only two-leggeds who have found them are the ones who know where to look.

You know where to look. Knowing the gifts that are inside you will help you learn to live from the heart.

"To know how to choose a path with heart is to learn how to follow the inner beat of intuitive feeling. Logic can tell you superficially where a path may lead . . . but it cannot judge whether your heart will be in it. It is worthwhile to scan every life choice with rational thinking, but wrong to base a life choice on it. Choosing whom to marry or what to do as a life work, or what principles to base one's life on require that one's heart be in the choice."

—JEAN SHINODA BOLEN, M.D.

YOUR PATH IS YOUR LIFE

In *The Teachings of Don Juan*, Carlos Castaneda responds to the burning question we all have, especially during our teen years: "What path do I take?" Don Juan's advice to Castaneda was as follows:

"Does this path have heart? If it does, the path is good; if it doesn't, it is of no use. Both paths lead nowhere; but one has a heart, the

"The soul would have no rainbow if the eyes had no tears."

—MINQUASSI SAYING

"Listening to a liar is like drinking warm water."

—NATIVE AMERICAN INDIAN SAYING (TRIBE UNKNOWN)

other doesn't. One makes for a joyful journey; as long as you follow it, you are one with it. The other will make you curse your life. One makes you strong; the other weakens you."

Don Juan's statement that "both paths lead nowhere" speaks to the truth that all paths really lead to the same end—our death. It isn't so much the *destination* that really matters but the *path* that you take. You are always on the path. You never really arrive anywhere and stay put! As soon as you are done with one thing, such as high school, you are right back on your path, always moving onward. So it is actually the path that you choose that matters most, and not so much where you believe you will end up. Whether Hailey went to a distant college after high school or took a year off was not as important as whether she followed her heart, her truth. You have so many choices at your age! I guarantee that choosing the "path with heart" will make those choices more effortless.

What really matters is how we live. Are you now, in your teen years, beginning to take a path with heart? To find the path with heart you need to follow your intuitive self. And to live from your heart you have to have courage! It takes courage and heart to become who you are intended to be. Humans are unique in this way. It takes an inner effort and commitment to *become* someone. Other living creatures don't have such *choices*—a sunflower seed becomes a full-grown sunflower, an eagle egg hatches an eagle, all without choice. Growth and being are automatic for all other creatures but humans. *Your* life is dependent upon the choices you make.

Don't allow fear to guide your choice of a path. When you let fear make choices for you, you take the path that appears safer but limits you in the end. Fear stops you from taking *necessary* risks—those actions that stretch you and open you up to your real potential. As you saw in chapter 6, you need to risk asking for what you want in order to manifest it.

Making Decisions with Heart

When there are important choices you are trying to make—bring your heart into it. Imagine bringing the decision down into your heart center. Let this choice live in your heart for a while instead of thinking you have to rush and make a decision. Steer clear of getting caught up in "yes, no, yes, no" thinking. This wrenches the heart and body. Instead, let your self not be sure. Even say to yourself or to others, "I'm not sure right now." Giving yourself permission not to be sure relaxes the heart and gives you room to make the best choice for yourself at the best time. As Hailey put it, "My path in life, which I was desperately trying to find, was inside me the entire time."

Heart Meditation

Mudra for heart meditation

This meditation is borrowed from the yoga tradition, and uses a classic hand posture, *mudra,* to encourage energy to flow from your heart. This hand posture, along with yogic breathing, awakens the heart and slows down the racing mind. You will find that this meditation has a calming effect as you open up to your heart.

Give yourself about five to ten minutes to do this meditation. Sit in a relaxed posture with your eyes closed. Bring your thumbs and forefingers together to form a triangle over your heart center (fourth chakra). Now inhale deeply through your nose and exhale through your mouth. Do eight of these breaths.

Repeat this series of breaths three times, resting after each series with a couple of regular breaths.

Lower your hands, while remaining focused on your heart center. Now ask yourself:

Am I on the path with heart? *or* Does this path I choose have heart?

Let the breath just breathe through you naturally as you allow an image or thought to come as a response to your question. Continue to breathe, and focus on listening to your heart and paying attention to the answer. Take a few moments to journal your experience.

Just asking the question from the heart is a great practice all by itself. Sometimes you will get a clear response to your question, while other times you will just need to live with the question for a while. When you don't get an answer while doing the meditation, carry the question out into your daily life with you. Live the question from the heart, and a clear answer will come.

Loving-kindness Meditation

The following meditation on loving-kindness is a 2,500-year-old practice that uses repeated expressions, feelings, and images to develop a loving heart toward ourselves and others.

Sit comfortably and slowly close your eyes. Let your body relax more than you would in the breath meditations. Let yourself be comfortable and rested. As best you can, let your mind rest, letting go of the worries or planning that often goes on. Take a few minutes to bring your awareness to your breath . . . bringing your awareness more and more into this time of meditation. Notice the various sensations in the body. Continue to relax and bring your awareness to your breathing and body.

Then imagine breathing into your heart. On each breath imagine your heart softening and opening. And say quietly to yourself:

> *May I be filled with loving-kindness.*
> *May I be strong and happy.*
> *May I feel good about myself.*
> *May all my dreams come true.*

Imagine each cell, molecule, and atom in your body filling up with the meaning of these words. Repeat these phrases again and again, letting the meaning fill you up. Continue to breathe in and out these words of love for yourself. Feel your heart open up to you.

Then begin to include others in the room, or others in your life you care about. Imagine your heart opening up and sending some of this loving-kindness and well wishing to everyone near to your heart. Bring to mind all the people you love and care about. Say these phrases softly to them:

> *May you be filled with loving-kindness.*
> *May you be strong and happy.*
> *May you feel good about yourself.*
> *May all your dreams come true.*

Send them this love, while always keeping some for yourself. This keeps you replenished. Include friends, neighbors, teachers, animals, people you know who are suffering and need your loving thoughts.

Imagine sending it anywhere and everywhere.

Try including someone you're angry with. How does it feel to send him or her these kind thoughts and loving feelings?

Now sit softly in your breath for a while as you fill yourself and the world with your love and kindness.

As you practice this meditation you will experience a deeper and deeper connection to yourself and to others. At first, it may feel awkward or difficult—this is quite common. Keep practicing it, and soon you will find yourself feeling more love for yourself and for others. As Shinzen Young reminds us:

> **"There are two main goals in the spiritual life. One is to have a sense of complete freedom and fulfillment for oneself. The other is to be a source of love and goodwill to others. If you can experience negativity (anger, hate, jealousy) as *energy*, and 'recolor' that energy as love and goodwill, and let it spread out from you, then you will be simultaneously achieving those two goals. With practice, any person can experience a freedom through such a practice."**

"The more you ask how far you have to go, the longer your journey seems."

—Seneca Indian proverb

"Perhaps the earth can teach us as when everything seems to be dead in winter and later proves to be alive."

—Pablo Neruda, Chilean poet

Living more and more from your heart chakra will practically guarantee that you will call to you authentic friendships and intimate, safe relationships. Bringing forth your true nature through the exercises and practices in this book will also result in a life filled with positive friendships, worthwhile work, and a passionate love life. All these promises rely on your willingness to continue to open yourself up, to commit to the intuitive life, a life that encourages you to bring forth your true nature and live from the heart.

A Model for Changing

You really can change anything that is not working for you in your life. You can change your luck. You can change your chances for a loving, caring relationship. You can change just about anything with this powerful and proven method.

I use the word *change* with some hesitation. That is because the goal here is not really to *change* yourself as much as it is to bring forth your true nature. Pema Chodron points out that our need to change ourselves all the time is a form of self-hatred. Always wanting to modify ourselves is not a kind or healthy attitude. Ms. Chodron recommends instead that we befriend ourselves—beginning with accepting ourselves, warts and all. Self-acceptance is a form of true love. It is not your true nature that you want to change, but the *obstacles* to this true nature.

You can apply this four-step process to anything you want to change in your life.

1. *Acceptance.* Name what it is that is not working. Accept that this is what is causing the problem in your life.
2. *Responsibility.* Blaming others needs to cease completely. If you see your problem as somebody else's fault, then only that person holds the power to change the situation. Be responsible for your own part in the problem. This alone will give you the power to change it.
3. *Discipline.* You have to be willing to do things differently—to break from comfortable habits and familiar behavior.
4. *Change.* Going through the first three steps creates change in the Rainbow Body—it will *feel* different.

Now pick one thing to change and apply this model. Start with just one, so you can easily track its success.

Never Give Up Hope

It is difficult to see the path with heart, or to do much of anything positive for ourselves, if we are feeling hopeless. To have short periods of feeling hopeless is part of the human condition. But when you begin to have long periods of hopelessness you can end up in serious trouble. Getting stuck in the muck of hopelessness often results in depression and drug addictions (you use drugs to feel better, but this works only *temporarily*).

Our culture can foster feelings of hopelessness by not encouraging you to take care of yourself or to follow your heart's truth. This high-tech, fast-paced world, where the focus is more on the destination than the path, often overlooks matters of the heart. We are rushed at an early age—off to school in the morning, only to rush from one class to another. (I am often told by students that they are only given a few minutes to get from one class to another, even when it is on the other side of the campus.) All this rushing makes it very difficult to become quiet and still enough to check in with ourselves, our hearts. We can't do the processes in this book, or even connect with our hearts, while driving down the highway talking on the cell phone.

As I pointed out earlier in the book, it is important to honor our own timing—being rushed through our lives interferes with our true nature. Therefore, to get in touch with ourselves, to feel once again connected to hope and to our path, we need to slow down. And *breathe*. There is a way through the hopelessness if you just stop and take time for yourself. You can *always* find an answer. The truth is: You *can* help yourself. *The truth is, there is always hope.*

"When at some point in our lives, we meet a real tragedy—which could happen to any one of us—we can react in two ways.

Obviously we can lose hope, let ourselves slip into discouragement, into alcohol, drugs, unending sadness. Or else we can wake ourselves up, discover in ourselves an energy that was hidden there, and act with more clarity, more force."
—His Holiness the 14th Dalai Lama, *Violence and Compassion*

Even though the last thing you may want to do is to reach out—*reach out.* Doing so is a way to say no to the hopelessness. It says, "I may not be able to see a way out right now, but I know there has to be one." The best way out of feelings of hopelessness is creating solutions—coming up with ideas and options, and a good friend or trusted adult can help with this.

In the Name of Love

When we speak of a path with heart, the word *love* is bound to come to mind. But what does it really mean? So many things are said and done in the name of love. A child is ridiculed in the name of love: *I say this for your own good.* People try to control and possess each other in the name of love: *I don't want you to move away because I love you.* People even kill in the name of love! *Love* is such a misused word that its true meaning has been lost.

When someone says "I love you," what love means to him or her could vary greatly from what it means to you! My spiritual teacher suggests that we change the word *love* to *affinity.* To have an *affinity* for someone is to regard and respect this other person as a unique and precious individual. Affinity is an expression of true caring from the heart without a need for the other to behave a certain way.

Love is such a loaded word that it generates a tremendous amount of psychic energy. That is what often makes it so hard to see the

**"Something we were withholding made us weak
Until we found out it was ourselves."**
—Robert Frost,
American poet

"If you always do what you always did, you will always get what you always got."
—Author Unknown

truth about love. What has love looked like in your life? Spend some time thinking about the following questions, and journal your responses if you like.

> What has been done to you, or by you, in the name of love?
>
> Do those who say they love you respect your individuality?
>
> Do you hold an affinity (a respect and caring) for yourself?
>
> Do you have a true affinity for those whom you claim love?

The Truth about True Love

Is it possible to experience "true love"? Yes, but it may not look exactly like you might expect it to. Many psychologists and healers refer to it as "conscious love." Now that you are making your own choices about relationships, a healthy and realistic model of true love can help you make decisions that are right for you.

The most important ingredient in true love is *individual growth*. Yes! If you love someone, and someone loves you, you will encourage each other's individual growth. This holds true throughout your life. You will support each other's dreams and goals and allow room to change and grow. Whether the person you love is a friend, parent, or lover, inevitably you have to let that person go to do things that are important to him or her. True love, *conscious love*, supports your loved one's individual growth and personal empowerment.

For couples, true love encompasses more than just an infatuation or attraction to someone. It includes all of these qualities:

> personal freedom for both people
>
> good communication on all levels—verbal, energetic, emotional

"The longing for love and the movement of love is underneath all of our activities. The happiness we discover in life is not about possessing or owning or even understanding. Instead, it is the discovery of this capacity to love, to have a loving, free, and wise relationship with all of life. Such love is not possessive but arises out of a sense of our own well-being and connection with everything."

—JACK KORNFIELD, BUDDHIST TEACHER, TAKEN FROM *A PATH WITH HEART*

individual space

responsible behavior toward yourself and the other

personal empowerment

affinity and friendship

compatible goals (but not necessarily the same goals)

caring

bliss (at times)

delight in one another

an ability to say no, and to say yes

allowing the other to be negative as well as positive

there is no coercion by either person

the relationship is nonpossesive

each person understands the basis of their attraction

the relationship is based in truth, not fantasy

both people's needs are respected

knowing when it is time to move on and say good-bye

True love is more than just wanting that person to be "the one." When you do fall in love, how can you tell you have found the right person?

Is This Person Right for Me?

Have you ever gotten into a relationship and awakened one day wondering why you were with this person and how you got in so deep? I have! Usually this happened when I thought the person was special for superficial reasons and I was caught up in trying to get the other person to like me. I didn't take the time to really see this other person and to notice how I felt in my Rainbow Body when I was with him. I didn't

> "Sometimes a firm 'no' or 'I can't' or 'I won't allow that; it is beyond my limit' is the most spiritual thing we can say."
> —JACK KORNFIELD, BUDDHIST PSYCHOLOGIST, AUTHOR OF *A PATH WITH HEART*

really take the time to find out if *I* liked *him*—I was too concerned with whether or not he liked me. I did this with friendships, too.

What you really want is to be in a relationship with someone you truly care about, who truly cares about you. So how do you know this is really the case in your relationship? You may have learned already that the *accepted* signs of affection are not so reliable—gift giving, compliments, attentiveness, spending time together. You may have known someone who was good at giving gifts or complimenting you but didn't really care about you. So can you find out if your relationship is genuine? Yes! By learning to listen to your heart.

"If you have the honesty to pray for real, from the heart, you will be heard."
—Wounye' Waste' Win, Lakota Medicine Woman

Listening with Your Heart

Begin by developing more awareness of your heart chakra. Practice "listening" and noticing from this place. Rather than focusing all the energy from your *head*, have your attention come from your heart. *This engages the energy of the heart chakra*—love, care, compassion, and attentiveness to the Rainbow Body. (Remember to have your second chakra connected with your heart chakra.) This is a very important practice that helps connect the energies of these two chakras—sexuality and compassion—together. Simply visualize a cord connecting your second chakra with your heart chakra (see page 81).

The next time you are with someone you are attracted to, bring your awareness to your heart chakra. You can even place your hand on your heart center. Ask yourself, Does this person care about me? Notice how it feels in your body when you ask this. Stay aware and present. Breathe.

Don't be willing to drift off, unaware. If you really want to find out what is true between the two of you, don't use alcohol or drugs on a date. This really messes with your perceptions! Your intuition is dormant when you are high, and all those desires of wanting this to be the right person take over.

Be alert to signs that you are resistant to even knowing whether or not this is the real thing! Sometimes we don't want to ask a question if we are afraid of the answer. Whatever you hear when you listen with your heart, the power is yours to decide what to do about it. It is always your choice who you will have a relationship with and who you will not. When you are willing to look at the truth within you—in your intuitive, energy body—you will find that you don't get in harmful or possessive relationships.

An important energy tip: When you are exploring relationships, tuning in to the energy of a situation or person will help you choose true love and true friendships. The energy of another person *always* tells the truth. When the words don't match the energy—*trust the energy.* Pay attention to this, so you won't end up believing something that isn't true. Practice noticing when the energy does match the person's words and when it doesn't. And *always trust the energy.*

Possessive Love: Not the Real Thing!

It is all too easy to confuse possessive love with true love. You may believe that someone who wants to know everything you think and do is expressing love; that someone who wants to spend all of his or her time with you loves you; that someone who wants to take care of you by making decisions for you loves you. But this is not true love. This is possessive love.

Possessive love will always harm and undermine you. Being possessed is the opposite of being personally empowered. (Reflect back to the third chakra exercises in personal empowerment in chapter 3.)

"Power over others is weakness disguised as strength. True power is within, and it is available to you now."

—ECKHART TOLLE, AUTHOR OF *THE POWER OF NOW*

In a possessive relationship you have to give up parts of yourself. You give up your ability and your right to determine things for yourself (including ending the relationship).

People who need to possess are often afraid of being alone. They tend to "grab" someone they think they love and not let go. They will use power to control someone, rather than empowering themselves and their partner. Possessive love is not necessarily about physical power—but rather about *emotional and energetic power over another person.* In a possessive relationship there is always an unbalanced energy interchange. Possessive people deplete you of your energy.

An Oglala elder once told me that "a frog does not drink up the pond in which he lives." She was speaking of all the young women she knew who were letting themselves be "drunk up" by the young men they were in a relationship with. (This can go both ways— there are many stories of young women possessing young men.) Possessive love is abusive (in the name of love) and it robs you of your life energy. It drinks up the very pond in which you live and then greedily leaves you behind and moves on to another pond. True love does not drain you of your energy or life essence. It is *never* abusive.

Sure signs that you are in a possessive relationship:

- The other person needs to have a say in everything, or most everything, that you do.
- He or she does not give you time to think for yourself and demands immediate decisions.
- You find you are frequently unsure and you let the other person make up your mind for you.
- You spend most, if not all, of your time with this person.
- He or she does not like your friends.

- He or she threatens to leave you if you exert any independence.
- He or she is jealous of your family and/or friends.
- Whenever this person is around, you give your power over to him or her.
- You are losing energy and enthusiasm you had for past interests.
- You find you do things with this person that you said you didn't want to do.

The more of these statements that are true, the more possessive and dangerous the relationship is. But even if you only recognize one of these as true for you, you may be in a possessive relationship. As long as you are willing to be in this kind of relationship, you will stifle your true nature and true love will elude you. Even true love found in friendships and family relationships is nonpossessive and empowering.

Changing a Negative Belief about Yourself

Of course, if you are full of self-loathing or just don't care much about yourself, experiencing true love will be nearly impossible. Do you hold some negative, even harmful beliefs about yourself? Negative beliefs hold great power over us because they are accompanied by strong feelings, images, and *energy*. If they were just thoughts, then maybe they would just float on by, unnoticed. But these negative beliefs carry such potent energy that they are impossible to ignore.

To change a negative belief you hold about yourself takes more than just repeating a simple affirmation. You need to deal with the *energy* of a given belief, too. When you want to free yourself from a

"In the beginning, there is struggle and a lot of work for those who come near to God. But after that, there is indescribable joy. It is just like building a fire: at first it's smoky and your eyes water, but later you get the desired result. Thus we ought to light the Divine fire in ourselves with tears and effort."

—AMMA SYNCLETICA, EGYPTIAN HERMITESS, WRITER

"Just as we can't stop birds from flying over our heads, but can stop them from nesting in our hair, so we can't avoid evil thoughts, but we can stop them from taking root in our heart and giving birth to evil deeds."

—MARTIN LUTHER, GERMAN REFORMATION LEADER

"Our first teacher is our own heart."

—CHEYENNE SAYING

negative picture of yourself, practice the following exercise. This will help release the negative energy from your Rainbow Body as well as release the feelings and images that go with this negative picture you have of yourself.

"Ask questions from your heart and you will be answered from the heart."

—OMAHA PROVERB

"With all things and in all things, we are relatives."

—SIOUX PROVERB

Take a moment to ground. Then lie down on the floor in a comfortable position, with your neck supported by a pillow. Remember to breathe and do it with little effort. Bring to mind the negative belief you hold about yourself. Is it about your body size? Is it about how you think the opposite sex sees you? Do you perceive yourself as lazy, or dull, or, "too brainy?" For a moment hold the negative thought in your mind. For example: "Things never work out for me" or "I am too brainy." Then, as you attempt to hold this belief in your mind, imagine filling your entire Rainbow Body with LOVE. Fill up every molecule, every atom, every cell with the energy and intention of love. Infuse the negative belief with the energy of love. Begin to breathe rapidly, with no gap between the in breath and the out breath. Do this breathing for only two minutes. When finished with the two minutes of rapid breathing, relax and enjoy the energy that is in your body.

This exercise is borrowed from rebirthing techniques and the Toltec tradition (Mexican shamanic practices) of freeing ourselves energetically from negative belief patterns. Do this routinely (once a day) with any negative concept you hold of yourself, until you notice that you no longer hold this belief. This also opens up the heart energy, and moves it throughout your entire Rainbow Body.

DOING FOR OTHERS

Although this book *is* all about you—you bringing forth your true nature, you listening and acting on your intuition, you living the path with heart—your efforts will have an impact on many others. Living the path with heart will not only benefit you but will also benefit everyone you encounter. Your truth will be like a rock dropped into the middle of a lake—creating ripples that move outward across the entire lake until they reach the shore. You will even have an impact on people you never meet. It matters a great deal to me, and to everyone else, that you bring forth all the love and power that is inside of you.

As you focus on your own journey, you can extend the benefit of your efforts beyond yourself by reciting a dedication prayer for the happiness of others. Every time you are done with a given meditation or practice, you can recite this Tibetan prayer-dedication. You may invent another prayer that works for you or borrow from the many prayers that are used throughout the various spiritual traditions. By offering this prayer at the completion of your personal spiritual practices, you are then dedicating these efforts to benefit all of humanity. Ideally, every act we make, every choice we make, and every exercise we practice can be dedicated in this way, becoming a blessing to everyone.

DEDICATION PRAYER

Through the power and truth of this practice
May all beings have happiness
and the causes of happiness.
May all be free from sorrow and the causes of sorrow.

May we all never be separated from our sacred happiness
which is sorrowless.
And may we all live in equanimity
without fear and addiction
And live believing in the equality of all living things.

And from me to you—

Through the Power and truth of this practice
May you have happiness.
May your life be free from sorrow and the causes of sorrow.
May you live in freedom
without fear and addiction
And live knowing you are loved and appreciated.

**"I sought my soul
And the soul I could not
see.
I sought my God
And God eluded me.
I sought my brother
And I found all three."**

—PRAYER, AUTHOR UNKNOWN

Meeting Your Future Self: A Meditation

You do have a big, mysterious, and beautiful future that awaits you. Okay, okay, there will probably be times of difficulty and, for some, great challenges. Yet the future is bright—trust me on this. Not one of my difficulties or challenges stopped me from having a big, beautiful life, and yours won't stop you either. If you are having doubt about your future self, take some time and do this meditation. Have someone read it out loud, or record it and listen to the tape. Give yourself ten to fifteen minutes for this meditation. You may be seated or lying down in a comfortable position for this journey.

Close your eyes and notice your breathing. Just let the breath move by itself . . . Begin to follow your breath in and out of your nostrils, noticing how it brushes against the top of your nostrils as it moves in and moves out . . . With each exhalation let your body relax . . . relax and breathe . . . Now imagine yourself in your favorite place in nature. Notice the soft white of a few clouds passing by in the blue sky . . . Breathe and relax . . . Now notice that way, way off in the distance an adult is approaching you. This adult that you cannot really see yet is you. The adult "you" is walking toward you, has come back to visit with you and to let you know that your future awaits you . . . This adult "you" has reached his or her full potential . . . Your adult self is full of wisdom, and trusts and acts on your intuition. Let this adult "you" come closer, and stand together in this place in nature that you so enjoy . . . Notice how he or she looks . . . strong and beautiful, self-assured. Begin to talk with him or her, and ask whatever it is you would like to know about your future self. Notice and take in all that you are shown . . . You may see scenes from your future life. Just notice and ask any questions you may have. Reach out and touch this future self, feel the texture and warmth of your adult skin . . . Spend two to five minutes asking your questions, experiencing this future self.

Then say good-bye to your future self and let her or him return back to the future . . . Let your adult self go, knowing you can bring her or him back anytime to visit. Now begin again to notice yourself there alone in your favorite place in nature, feeling stronger and more confident about yourself and your future . . . Return your awareness to your breath, noticing how it moves in and out. Feel your body on the floor and silently count to ten. Gradually open your eyes and sit up slowly. Take some time to share your experience with someone or write in your journal about your visit with your future self.

"If you want the world to become loving and compassionate, become loving and compassionate yourself."

—GARY ZUKAV,
THE SEAT OF THE SOUL

"Oh, may this be the one who
will bring forth
the good, true and beautiful in our
family lineage;
Oh, may this be the one who will
break the harmful
family patterns or harmful nation patterns."

—ANGELES ARRIEN, *THE FOUR-FOLD WAY*

9
Not the End,
but the Beginning
Wisdom for the Road

⊚ THE AUTHOR'S ENCOUNTER WITH HIS HOLINESS, ⊚
THE DALAI LAMA

I didn't have much love in my childhood or as a teenager, and this lack of love made my heart somewhat frozen and scared. Even though I began practicing meditation at the age of sixteen, I believe a part of my heart was always shut off. But an encounter with His Holiness, the Dalai Lama, changed that forever.

His Holiness is the spiritual and political leader of the exiled Tibetan people. He is revered throughout the world for spreading the message of compassion and loving-kindness. I attended a reception for him at the Unitarian Church in Madison, Wisconsin, where I was among about one hundred others milling around in the church as we awaited his arrival. We were all offered tea and cakes as we waited. I could feel the emotions rising up in the room and in myself. We all seemed to want something from His Holiness.

**On the way to God the
difficulties
Feel like being ground by
a millstone,
Like night coming at
noon, like
Lightning through the
clouds.
But don't worry!
What must come, comes.
Face everything with
love,
As your mind dissolves in
God."**

—LAL DED, KASHMIRI MYSTIC

*Finally he arrived, and a path was cleared for him to make his way to
the podium. By sheer luck I found myself right beside the path where His
Holiness would pass! Here was my chance to be near him! Then I felt a
light shove from behind me. Everyone was crowding toward the path. The
man behind me was holding flowers to give to His Holiness. He eagerly
reached past me with his gift, thrusting the flowers in front of my face.*

*As the man shouted out "Your Holiness! Your Holiness!" and held his
flowers out toward the approaching Dalai Lama, I remembered what this
was really all about. It was not about getting recognized by His Holiness.
It was not about being heard or even being seen by His Holiness. It was
about love. It was all about kindness and generosity. It was about taking
every opportunity that arises to express these truths. This is what people
like His Holiness were trying to teach us. So I stepped back and let the
man behind me be in front and nearer to His Holiness.*

*As I stepped back and stood behind the man with flowers, His
Holiness walked by. As he did, he reached out his arm past the man with
the flowers, and squeezed my shoulder and smiled at me. The love I felt
in that moment instantly woke up more love that was buried in my heart.
I was filled with joy!*

*We listened as His Holiness talked about helping the Tibetan people,
and about all of us being good to one another. When he was ready to
leave, we had to make another path for him. I ended up on the other side
of the path, again right on its edge. I stood there, happy to be close to him
again and filled with love. Then a woman behind me began to cry out
and push me: "Your Holiness, your Holiness . . ." She really wanted to be
near him. So, again I backed away and let her stand in front of me. And
once again, as His Holiness walked by, he reached around this woman
and squeezed my shoulder and smiled at me.*

*What a lesson I learned! What a blessing I received. And it wasn't
about His Holiness knowing me by name, or even acknowledging me.*

Somehow, he saw my heart, my kindness, and returned it with his touch. Because I opened up my heart to love, love walked in and gave me a gentle squeeze.

I don't know if the man with the flowers or the pleading woman got what they wanted. I hope so. But I left with a more open heart and a lesson well learned: that when I send out loving-kindness and generosity, I will receive those very things in return. I also learned that there will be times when it may appear as if I am giving up something (my spot in the line) but really I am opening up to something greater.

A Story of Tibetan Wisdom
retold by Jack Kornfield

At Buddhist "initiations" or "empowerments" a learned teacher will empower the attendees with certain energies, such as compassion, love, and courage. Tibetan Buddhists are known to use many forms of visualizations in their spiritual practice. Skilled practitioners are known to manifest what they visualize as realistically as what we experience in the physical world.

One day, a great lama was giving an initiation to a large gathering, and a young woman came to receive the empowerment. It meant a great deal to this young woman to leave her home and travel alone to receive this lama's empowerment.

In Tibet it is customary to give a gift to the lama at the end of such an empowerment as a token of appreciation. This young woman had a kilo of fresh yak butter to offer, one of the favored means of exchange in Tibet. It was a great deal of butter for this young woman with such meager resources to give away. She was holding it carefully under her jacket, and she planned to offer it to the master after receiving his blessing.

There came a time in the ceremony when the lama would ordinarily

"Experience, with its wounds worn like trophies, longs to pass on its hard-won wisdom."

—Louise Carus Mahdi, counselor, wilderness adventure guide for teens

"Never spend time with people who don't respect you."

—Maori proverb

touch each disciple on the head with a sacred vessel filled with nectar. But because there were so many people gathered before him, he simply instructed them all to visualize the vase he was holding on his head, and imagine him placing it atop each of their heads.

The faithful young woman did exactly as instructed and received the empowerment in its entirety. But when the rite was completed, and it was time to offer her precious butter to the revered master, she stood up and uttered—in a voice sounding like the lama, and echoing his very words— "Now simply visualize, venerable lama, that you are receiving as my offering this kilo of fresh butter that you see in my hand!"

And then, laughing to herself, she made her way home, a stronger, wiser, and wealthier young woman indeed, with the butter tucked snugly under her arm.

"I distinguish excellent teachers by several criteria. They are, above all else, inspired. Their ideas and Beingness exalt and uplift anyone who may come in contact with them."

—W. BRUGH JOY, M.D., FROM *JOY'S WAY*

RECOMMENDATIONS FOR THE ROAD

You are about to go on the road trip of your life! This of course refers to your journey into your full independence, but it is also a metaphor for developing and making the most of your intuitive and spiritual powers. I wish for you a safe and beautiful journey and offer these recommendations as you venture out beyond the pages of this book.

If you have found this book helpful (all or some of it), great. But this book is not enough for you. I want you to put it down for a while and go in search of a spiritual teacher—a transpersonal psychotherapist, psychic healer, or mentor, or a spiritually focused class (sangha, yoga), so you can receive *personal* instruction. All the teachings in this book come from my heart to yours. However, I could not have afforded these teachings to you had I not received years of individual guidance from those who instructed me. My teachers included Tibetan lamas, a psychic development class, a vipassana sangha (Buddhist meditation group), American Buddhist teachers, an acupuncturist, a psychic healer, a craniosacral practitioner, and an excellent psychotherapist. Without these grounded and gifted teachers, this book would not be in your hands. The material in this book will become even more real for you when you find your own teachers and groups.

In Search of a Spiritual Teacher: What to Look For

I found my first teachers in the books I read: Stephen Levine, author of *A Gradual Awakening*; W. Brugh Joy, M.D., author of *Joy's Way*; and John A. Sanford, who wrote *The Kingdom Within*. Then I went in search of flesh-and-blood teachers. Fortunately, I encountered safe, skillful, and dynamic mentors, but you should be aware that some spiritual teachers can do you harm. Before you commit to working with a healer or teacher, pay attention to which way the power—the energy—is going. Notice how you feel when you are with this person—drained or empowered? Strengthened or weakened? Hopeful or hopeless? Give yourself time to decide whether this person is the right teacher for you.

A good spiritual teacher will fill you with a sense of what is possible for you. He or she will build you up, not tear you down. Although good spiritual teachers may challenge some of your beliefs and decisions, they won't do this in a way that makes you feel inferior. Whenever I was working with my spiritual teachers I noticed how they made room for all of the participants to feel their own personal power. Although my teachers were more knowledgeable than I was in a given area, I never felt small or unimportant. I knew that my power was also felt and honored by them. Even when they told me things that were hard to hear (such as, "You are in a bad situation, and you need to change it"), I never felt put down. To this day I

"The greatest and simplest power of a teacher is the environment of their own freedom."
—JACK KORNFIELD, BUDDHIST MEDITATION TEACHER

"The wisdom teacher has verified these teachings through his own experience and, motivated by compassion, speaks to the student from the realization he has in his heart."
—JAMGÖN KONGTRUL THE GREAT, AUTHOR OF *THE TEACHER-STUDENT RELATIONSHIP*

continue to learn from some teachers in person, as well as many others through their writing.

Look for a psychic healer or spiritual teacher who:

has had professional training

has a good, proven reputation

has been recommended by someone you trust

has clear boundaries with you and does not ask favors from you

refers you to other practitioners who can help you, such as a therapist, chiropractor, support group, or homeopath

offers guidance to help you to make the best decisions for yourself, rather than making decisions for you and predicting your future

never asks for or expects sexual contact with you (even if you are of age to consent)

has a sense of humor and helps you to see the fun of it all

does not drain you of your energy, but whose energy is open and flowing *toward* you

builds on your strengths and makes you feel big and powerful. (If you feel yourself shrinking and getting small around a teacher, he or she may be on a power trip.)

does not claim to be the only one who can help you

does not force you to accept a particular belief system

does not pressure you to join a certain group

is not judgmental but has compassion and understanding for you and all others

allows the relationship to end when it is time

"In the lojong teachings the teacher is referred to as the spiritual friend, the *Kalyanamitra*. The teacher is like a senior warrior, or a student warrior who is further along the path. It is somebody who inspires you to walk the path of warriorship (spiritual truth) yourself. Looking at them reminds you of your own softness, your own clarity of mind, and your own ability to continually step out and open."
—PEMA CHÖDRÖN, AUTHOR OF *START WHERE YOU ARE*

Before you search for the right practitioner to work with, consider what it is you desire and expect from a spiritual teacher or spiritual experience. Get as clear about this as possible. If you are not clear about what you are looking for in a teacher or in a spiritual practice, you may accept someone else's agenda as your own. Of course, you may be unsure of what it is you want. So you may want to "try on" different ideas and practices for a fit. Even then, be clear that you are just checking out this Buddhist temple or this Christian group—without feeling pressured to join. *You* get to decide what group or teachings you want to be a part of, and *you* get to decide what fits for you and what doesn't fit. You may receive helpful advice and suggestions, but ultimately the spiritual path you choose should be based on your questions and needs about your life. As always, let your intuition and your Rainbow Body be your guide.

What to Look Out For: Spiritual Seduction

Unfortunately, there are spiritual teachers who only want to possess and control you. Watch out for those who want to seduce you spiritually. Spiritual seduction occurs when someone convinces you that he or she has all the answers, or claims a special relationship with you (therefore, you feel you owe that person sex, more money, etc). Spiritual seduction makes you feel dependent on this other person for spiritual nourishment, and this is wrong. While a spiritual teacher may introduce you to spiritual truths, the real nourishment comes from the spirit within you and your external spiritual source.

"I kept wanting to hang out with this yoga teacher because he seemed to like me so much and he always could tell me what I needed to do. He said we had 'karma' to work out together and that we had spent

"Healing has no cultural boundaries."

—DR. DOWA,
TIBETAN PHYSICIAN

"Give me knowledge, so I may have kindness for all."

—PLAINS INDIAN PROVERB

many lifetimes together. I felt so connected to him. Then, when he assumed we would have sex, I thought, 'Sure, it is just part of our karma, our relationship.' And besides, I didn't think he would do anything to hurt me. I was eighteen, so the choice was mine.

"The weird thing is, I felt I had to keep going back to him for more, yet I wasn't really feeling good about myself. I began to feel worse and worse about myself, which created this need for me to keep going to him for more. Then I met up with two other girls who felt the same way and were also having sex with him. I really crashed! I still haven't gone back to a yoga class and don't know if I ever can!"

—KIRSTEN, AGE 19

The Real Thing

In 1993 I attended a weeklong retreat given by Sogyal Rinpoche, a Tibetan teacher and author of the book *The Tibetan Book of Living and Dying*. I had just finished the book and I had the feeling it would be very important for me to attend this retreat. At least two hundred others had the same intuitive nudge.

Each day we would spend time receiving instructions from Sogyal Rinpoche and then spend the rest of the time practicing our meditations and chants. It was a very intense and empowering experience. Sogyal Rinpoche always brought lightheartedness into his teachings and ended each day with a loving-kindness meditation. Just being in his presence and the loving presence of the other teachers had a positive effect on me. Each day I was feeling stronger and surer of myself.

Tibetan Buddhists believe it is important for students to have personal contact with the teacher. They understand that the value of the teachings is often expressed through the unique qualities of the

---

Someone who sees you and does not laugh out loud, or fall silent, or explode in pieces, is nothing more than the cement and stone of his own prison."

—RUMI,
SUFI POET

teacher. One day near the end of the retreat, Sogyal spent the day meeting with each one of us individually. We stood in alphabetically formed lines to wait for our turn. There were at least thirty other "*J*s" in my line, and I was somewhere near the end. I watched as others walked up to be greeted by Sogyal. I couldn't imagine why this brief meeting would be so valuable until it was my turn to meet with him. I felt such a welcoming, such compassion from him that I could only breathe and let the tears quietly roll down my cheeks. He greeted me, and held my hands. He asked if I had any questions. I asked him about continuing the practice after the retreat was completed. He offered me a helpful answer and some words of encouragement. He mentioned something about my being of help to others. I not only didn't feel small in the presence of this wonderful teacher, but I felt my own beauty and power as a teacher in my own right. In that brief time with him I knew that he was just an ordinary man; yet I also knew that he was a very accomplished teacher who offered incomparable wisdom and compassion.

This is what it feels like to be around a safe and skillful teacher. You feel loved and you feel the beauty and strength inside yourself get lit up when you are around him or her. It does no good to put a teacher on a pedestal, above you somehow. It is better that he or she is available to you and can illuminate the truth that is inside of you.

No one owns spiritual truth. All spiritual wisdom is for everyone —it isn't anybody's property. A good, safe teacher can help you come to understand and use spiritual wisdom, but teachers are also students. Even though I teach this material to others, I am still learning; I am still a student. We are all students of life, of the Great Mystery. Fortunately, the adage "There are many roads to enlightenment" proves to be true. It's really about finding your own way, the way that is safe and powerful for you.

> "In fact, the outer teacher is none other than the spokesman of our inner teacher, he teaches us how to receive the message of our inner teacher, and how to realize the ultimate teacher within, restoring a belief and confidence in ourselves and thereby freeing us from the suffering that comes from not knowing our True Nature."
>
> —SOGYAL RINPOCHE, FROM *DZOGCHEN AND PADMASAMBHAVA*

Now go freely . . . and follow what calls you.

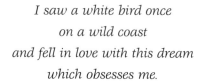

I saw a white bird once
on a wild coast
and fell in love with this dream
which obsesses me.

—AKIKO, JAPANESE POET

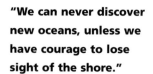

"We can never discover new oceans, unless we have courage to lose sight of the shore."

—ANDRÉ GIDE, FRENCH NOVELIST AND ESSAYIST

"What is REAL?" asked the Rabbit one day, when they were lying side by side . . .

"Does it mean having things that buzz inside of you and a stick out handle?"

"Real isn't how you are made," said the Skin Horse. "It's a thing that happens to you. When a child loves you for a long, long time, not just to play with, but REALLY loves you, then you become real."

"Does it hurt?" asked the Rabbit.

"Sometimes," said the Skin Horse, for he was always truthful. "When you are Real you don't mind being hurt."

"Does it happen all at once, like being wound up?" he asked, "or bit by bit?"

"It doesn't happen all at once . . . You become. It takes a long time. That's why it doesn't often happen to people who break easily, or have sharp edges, or who have to be carefully kept. Generally, by the time you are Real, most of your hair has been loved off, and your eyes drop out and you get loose in the joints and very shabby. But these things don't matter at all because once you are Real you can't be ugly, except to people who don't understand."

—MARGERY WILLIAMS, *THE VELVETEEN RABBIT*

Resources for Your Journey

To contact the author:

Flaming Rainbow Rites
Julie Tallard Johnson, LCSW
P.O. Box 186
Spring Green, WI 53588
(608) 963-0724
e-mail: Jewelhrt8@aol.com
Intuitive training and spiritual empowerment for all ages; meditation instruction; training on use of the I Ching; Senior Rites of Passage groups; resources for teens and those working with teens. Mending the Sacred Hoop workshops for teens and parents of teens. Flyer available.

Psychic Resources

Council on Spiritual Practices
www.csp.org
Focuses on direct, personal experience of the divine, rather than giving spiritual power away to practitioners. Promotes the practice of proven, safe, and well-researched spiritual experiences. Includes code of ethics for spiritual guides.

Intuition Network
www.intuition.org
A nonprofit organization. According to its mission statement, "The purpose of the Intuition Network is to help create a world in which all people feel encouraged to cultivate and use their inner intuitive resources."

The Positive Radio Network
Linda Mackenzie, C.H.T., Ph.D.
P.O. Box 385
Manhattan Beach, CA 90267
(310) 546-8523 Fax: (310) 545-4364
www.healthylife.net
e-mail: info@healthylife.net
Internet radio shows including Saturday-morning teen shows. The radio show offers "all-positive mind-body-spirit talk and original music." Linda is a great resource when searching for a psychic healer. She has a psychic code of ethics for all psychic healers to practice by.

Multicultural Spiritual Resources

Ancient Wisdom Spring
Sobonfu Somé
5960 South Land Park Drive #200
Sacramento, CA 95822-3313
(916) 446-5536
www.Sobonfu.com
e-mail: Sobonfu@aol.com
Workshops, rituals, tapes, and books by Sobonfu Somé. Focus is on ancient African teachings.

Bear Tribe Medicine Society
Bear Tribe Publishing
P.O. Box 959
Canandauqua, NY 14424
(585) 657-6881
Multiracial network of people offering medicine wheel gatherings, vision quests, and other programs.

Bear Tribe Medicine Society, Alabama
Wind Daughter, Medicine Chief
The Bear Tribe
PMB 223
3750–A Airport Blvd.
Mobile, AL 36608–1618
(251) 665-0499
www.ewebtribe.com

B'nai B'rith Youth Organization
www.bbyo.org
BBYO is a youth-led, worldwide organization that provides opportunities for Jewish youths to develop their leadership potential, a positive Jewish identity, and commitment to their personal development.

Gampo Abbey
Leaving Home and Becoming Homeless: A Monastic Youth Darhum
Pleasant Bay, Nova Scotia, Canada BOE 2PO
(902) 224-2752
www.gampoabbey.org
e-mail: gampo@shambhala.org
A monthlong temporary monastic program for young adults 17–25. The abbey also offers many other retreat and workshop options.

Hindu Resources Online
www.hindu.org
For information on Hinduism, check out this site brought to you by publishers of *Hinduism Today* Magazine.

JAYA
3210 Cross St.
Madison, WI 53711
Beth Wortzel and Jim Powell, musicians and licensed psychotherapists
e-mail: Mimosa@chorus.net
Beth and Jim offer popular classes and workshops on chanting, the power of vibration and sound, coming of age ceremonies for teens and families, meditation instruction. Will go into classrooms. CDs available for sale.

Shambhala Mountain Center
4921 County Road 68C
Red Feather Lakes, CO 80545-9505
www.shambhalamountain.org
(970) 881-2184
An ideal rural setting in a mountain valley for meditation, yoga, retreats, and workshops. Offers a variety of programs from many leaders in Tibetan Buddhism and other well-established spiritual practices. A great place to learn to meditate. Work studies are available.

Sufi Order International
www.sufiorder.org
"The human soul is continually seeking to realize its true being and fulfill its purpose in life." Resources, information, and books on Sufism. Includes links.

Sunray Meditation Society
Dhyani Ywahoo
P.O. Box 269
Bristol, VT 05443
(802) 453-4610
www.sunray.org
sunray@sover.net
Dhyani is a respected teacher in the Etoway Cherokee tradition and a master of Tibetan Buddhism. Sunray is an international society of people dedicated to planetary peace. They are

composed of three schools: Native American studies, Buddhist studies, and healing arts. Offers spiritual training. Refer to Web site for updates on programs.

Unitarian Universalist Association
www.uua.org
With historical roots in the Jewish and Christian traditions, UU is a liberal religion. It encompasses an openness to world religions and ancient practices. It is does not ask anyone to subscribe to a certain creed or belief. Most local groups have wonderful youth services. The Web site will link you to a UUA near you.

Resources on Tibetan Medicine

www.dharma–haven.org
A directory of Tibetan resources, Tibetan medicine information, and Medicine Buddha Empowerments.

www.tibet.com/Med_Astro/index.html
Includes information and several addresses of Tibetan medical centers and clinics.

www.tibetanmedicine.com
Information and link to a clinic in New York.

Flower Essence Remedies Resources

Flower Essence Society
P.O. Box 459
Nevada City, CA 95959
(800) 548-0075
e-mail: mail@flowersociety.org
Contact for Bach Flower Essences and related resources. You may also find Bach Flower Essences and other flower essences at your local health food store.

Nature's Acres
E. 8984 Weinke Road
North Freedom, WI 53951
(800) 499-HERB
www.naturesacres-herbals.com
e-mail: natures@chorus.net
Certified organic herbs and flower essences. Brochure available.

Resources for Attending to the Rainbow Body

Barbara Brennan School of Healing
Barbara Brennan
500 NE Spanish River Blvd., Suite 108
Boca Raton, FL 33431-4559
(561) 620-8767; (800) 924-2564
Fax: (561) 620-9028
www.barbarabrennan.com
e-mail: bbsh.office@barbarabrennan.com
Barbara teaches Brennan Healing Science®, the art and science of healing. A list of graduates who perform Barbara Brennan healing services is available.

Chakra Seminars
Anodea Judith
708 Gravenstein Hwy N #109
Sebastopol, CA 95472
www.sacredcenters.com
Information and workshops offered by Anodea Judith, author of *Eastern Body, Western Mind: Psychology and the Chakra System.*

Holotropics
Grof Transpersonal Training
Stanislas Grof
38 Miller Avenue, PMB 158
Mill Valley, CA 94941
www.holotropic.com
e-mail: gtt@holotrophic.com
Trainings and workshops in transpersonal and depth psychology. Holotropic breathwork workshops (must be 18 to attend alone). Also offers workshops on chanting and holotropic breathwork.

Massage Schools
Locate a massage school near you and set up an appointment to receive a massage. The cost is usually minimal because students need to practice on someone. Only graduating students practice on others, so you will receive a massage from a trained student.

Natural Healers
www.naturalhealers.com
A Web site that includes a massage school directory, acupuncture schools, and other healing schools. Will help find a school near you.

World of Alternatives
www.worldofalternatives.com
An Internet directory of alternative healing medicine practices including yoga, craniosacral therapy, and Bach Flower Essences.

Resources on Shamanism

Dance of the Deer Foundation
Center for Shamanic Studies
P.O. Box 699
Soquel, CA 95073
(831) 475-9560
www.shamanism.com
e-mail: shaman@shamanism.com

Offers workshops and training on the Huichol Indian approach to shamanism.

The Foundation for Shamanic Studies
P.O. Box 1939
Mill Valley, CA 94942
(415) 380-8282
www.shamanism.org
e-mail: info@shamanismstudies.com
Resources, products, training and information on the study of shamanism.

Pathways Foundation for Peace and Healing
Myron Eshowsky
P.O. Box 33345
Cleveland, OH 44133
www.peacehealing.org
e-mail: myron@mwt.net
Myron travels around the world offering rituals and teachings on community building, shamanism, and peace. Offers group and individual instruction on shamanism. May be able to refer you to a local shamanic practitioner.

School of Lost Borders
P.O. Box 796
Big Pine, CA 93513
(760) 938-3333
www.schooloflostborders.com
e-mail: staff@schooloflostborders.com
A well-established program for teens to experience a four-day vision quest. I highly recommend it for those of you who want to experience your fearlessness and connection to all things.

College Opportunities

Burlington College
95 North Avenue
Burlington, VT 05401
(800) 862-9616
www.burlcol.edu

Draws upon ancient wisdom and modern science to offer an accredited undergraduate and associate program in transpersonal psychology, social ecology, film and cinema, and other traditional degree programs. May obtain education through a low-residency independent study or on campus. Distance learning available. May design own program. A well-established college.

Goddard College
123 Pitkin Road
Plainfield, VT 05667
(800) 468-4888
www.goddard.edu
Accredited undergraduate and master's-level programs. A distance learning program. Programs include: mind/body healing therapies; community and ecological health; women's health; botanical and nutritional health.

Institute of Transpersonal Psychology
744 San Antonio Road
Palo Alto, CA 94303
(650) 493-4430
www.itp.edu
A well-established university with a variety of exciting undergraduate and graduate programs.

Naropa University
2130 Aropahoe Avenue
Boulder, CO 80302
(303) 444-0202
www.naropa.edu
Undergraduate programs in Buddhist and Western psychology, transpersonal and humanistic psychology, and ecopsychology; somatic psychology. (Somatic psychology includes understanding the Rainbow Body.) Highly recommended. You would encounter in-depth many of the practices found in this book.

Spiritual Resources for Overcoming Addiction

RoundRiver Institute, LLC
Mark L. Taylor, MA CPC, CADC
P.O. Box 35
Genoa, WI 54632-0035
e-mail: round_river2000@yahoo.com
Public speaking to teens on overcoming drug addiction. Offers meditation, honoring the spiritual as a way to heal from drug and alcohol addiction. Newsletter available.

Seven Circles Foundation
P.O. Box 559
Laguanitas, CA 94938
(510) 236-3512
www.sevencircles.org
Sweat lodges for people in recovery and healing from addiction. Native American ceremonies, pipe ceremony, vision quest, and educational programs. Will come into your classroom for a presentation. A nonprofit organization dedicated to the preservation of Native American lifeways.

Magazines

Circle Magazine
Celebrating Nature, Spirit and Magic
Circle Sanctuary
P.O. Box 219
Mt. Horeb, WI 53572
(608) 924-2216
www.circlesanctuary.org
e-mail: Circle@mhtc.net
A Nature Spirituality quarterly. A great resource of ritual, pagan tradition, vision quests, and other nature ceremonies. Has a network of practitioners of nature medicine throughout the world. The center has a Shamanic Wiccan Church headquartered on a nature preserve near Mt. Horeb.

Shaman's Drum
*A Journal of Experiential Shamanism
and Spiritual Healing*
P.O. Box 270
Williams, OR 97544
(541) 846-1313
e-mail: sdrm@budget.net
A great magazine to learn more about shamanism and to hook up with various shamanic practitioners and workshops. The publisher is the Cross-Cultural Shamanism Network.

Shambhala Sun Magazine
1585 Barrington Street, Suite 300
Halifax, Nova Scotia, Canada BJ3 IZ8
(902) 423-2701
www.shambhalasun.com
e-mail: magazine@shambhalasun.com
Articles and resources on Tibetan Buddhism and related practices. Includes lists of practitioners and dharma centers. A great resource to find Buddhist teachers and centers.

Symbol Dictionaries and Books

Animal Wisdom: The Definitive Guide to the Myth, Folklore and Medicine Power of Animals, by Jessica Dawn Palmer, Thorsons, 2001.

Dictionary of Symbols: An Illustrated Guide to Traditional Images, Icons, and Emblems, by Jack Tresidder, Chronicle Books, 1998.

Love Is in the Earth: A Kaleidoscope of Crystals (updated), by Melody. Earth-Love Publishing House, 1995.
A reference book describing the metaphysical properties of the mineral kingdom. (This book can often be located at gem and bead stores.)

The Penguin Dictionary of Symbols, by Jean Chevalier and Alain Gheerbrant, translated by John Buchanan-Brown, 1996.

Tree Wisdom: The Definitive Guidebook to the Myth, Folklore and Healing Powers of Trees, by Jacqueline Memory Paterson, Thorsons, 1997.

The Woman's Dictionary of Symbols & Sacred Objects, by Barbara G. Walker, Harper & Row, 1988.

Books to Read To Further Your Practice

Anatomy of the Spirit, by Caroline Myss, Random House, 1997.
Goes more in-depth into the energies and lessons of each chakra.

Awakening the Buddha Within, by Lama Surya Das, Broadway Books, 1997.
An in-depth and enjoyable read on the practices of Tibetan Buddhism.

Conversations with God for Teens, by Neale Donald Walsch, Putnam, 1999.
A great book for those questioning their relationship with God. An example of psychic writing.

The Eagles' Gift, by Carlos Castanada, Simon & Schuster, 1982.

Earth Medicine: Revealing Hidden Teachings of the Native American Wheel, by Kenneth Meadows, Element, 1996.
A good resource on medicine wheels and other earth medicine (for example, the significance of the four compass directions).

The Gift: Poems by Hafiz the Great Sufi Master, translated by Daniel James Ladinsky, Penguin USA, 1999.
A delightful and provocative collection of poems.

A Gradual Awakening, by Stephen Levine, Anchor Books, 1989.

I Ching for Teens, by Julie Tallard Johnson, Bindu Books, 2001.
A guide to this ancient Chinese oracle written especially for teens. A great tool to enhance your own psychic self and connect with the Great Tao.

The Medicine Woman, by Lynn Anderson, Harper & Row, 1982.
A wonderful story of a woman who finds her power.

The Power of NOW: A Guide to Spiritual Enlightenment, by Eckhart Tolle, New World Library, 1999.
A book about his spontaneous awakening and the value and means of living in the present moment.

Shared Spirits: Wildlife and Native Americans, by Dennis L. Olson, Northwood Press, 1995.
Links you to the greater wisdom available to us all through stories, photographs, and commentary.

Start Where You Are: A Guide to Compassionate Living, by Pema Chödrön, Shambhala, 2001.

Tarot for Teens, by M. J. Abadie, Bindu Books, 2002.

The Wisdom of No Escape and the Path of Loving-Kindness, by Pema Chödrön, Shambhala, 2001.
This book, along with *Start Where You Are,* is great for cultivating personal power and fearlessness. Also a beginner's guide to the Tibetan lojong practice mentioned in this book.

Yoga for Teens, by Thia Luby, Clear Light Publishing, 1999.

Bibliography

ANOQCOU: Ceremony Is Life Itself, by gkised-tanamoogk and Frances Hancock, Asyarte Shell Press, 1993.

Ancient Voices, Current Affairs: The Legend of the Rainbow Warriors, by Steven McFadden, Bear & Company, 1992.

Animal Tales from Around the World, retold by Naomi Adler, Barefoot Books, 1996.

Animals of the Soul: Sacred Animals of the Oglala Sioux, by Joseph Epes Brown, Element Books, 1992.

The Aquarian Conspiracy: Personal and Social Transformation in the 1980s, by Marilyn Ferguson, J. P. Tarcher, Inc., 1980.

Birth of a Modern Shaman: A Documented Journey and Guide to Personal Transformation, by Cynthia Bend and Tayja Wiger, Llewellyn Publications, 1988.

Black Elk Speaks, by John G. Neihardt (Flaming Rainbow), University of Nebraska Press, 1988.

The Bridge of Stars: 365 Prayers, Blessings, and Meditations from Around the World, edited by Marcus Braybrooke, Thorsons, 2001.

The Bronze Cauldron: Myths and Legends of the World, by Geraldine McCaughrean, McElderry Books, 1998.

The Cherokee Full Circle: A Practical Guide to Ceremonies and Traditions, by J. T. Garrett and Michael Tlanusta Garrett, Bear & Company, 2002.

Crossroads: The Quest for Contemporary Rites of Passage, edited by Louise Mahdi, Nancy Gever Christopher, and Michael Meade, Open Court, 1996.

Developing Intuition: Practical Guidance for Daily Life, by Shakti Gawain, Nataraj Publishing, 2000.

The Dhammapada, translated by Ross Carter and Mahinda Palihawadana, Oxford University Press, 1987.

Dictionary of Native American Mythology, by Sam D. Gill & Irene F. Sullivan, Oxford University Press, 1992.

The Discipline of Hope, by Herbert Kohl, The New Press, 1998.

Dreams, by Lama Surya Das, Sounds True, 2000. (*Note:* This is a CD.)

Dzogchen and Padmasambhava, by Sogyal Rinpoche, Rigpa Fellowship, 1990.

Eastern Body, Western Mind: Psychology and the Chakra System, by Anodea Judith, Celestial Arts, 1996.

Emissary of Love: The Psychic Children Speak to the World, by James F. Twyman, Hampton Roads Publishing, 2002.

Emotional Intelligence, by Daniel Goleman, Bantam Books, 1995.

The Essential Chögyam Trungpa, edited by Carolyn Rose Gimian, Shambhala Publications, 1999.

Everyone Is Right: A New Look at Comparative Religion and its Relation to Science, by Roland Peterson, DeVorss & Company, 1986.

Flower Essence Repertory, published by the Flower Essence Society, 1986.

Folktales from Around the World, edited by Jane Yolen, Pantheon Books, 1986.

Folktales from India, edited by A. K. Ramanujan, Pantheon, 1991.

The Four-Fold Way: Walking the Paths of the Warrior, Teacher, Healer, and Visionary, by Angeles Arrien, HarperSanFrancisco, 1993.

The Gnostic Gospels, by Elaine Pagels, Random House, 1979.

Hands of Light: A Guide to Healing Through the Human Energy Field, by Barbara Ann Brennan, Bantam Books, 1988.

Honey From The Rock: An Introduction To Jewish Mysticism, by Lawrence Kusher, Jewish Lights Publishing, 2000.

Healing the Shame That Binds You, by John Bradshaw, Health Communications, 1988.

I Ching for Teens, by Julie Tallard Johnson, Bindu Books, 2002.

In Search of Brazil's Quantum Surgeon: The Dr. Fritz Phenomenon, by Masao Maki, Cadence Books, 1997.

Intuitive Living: A Sacred Path, by Alan Seale, Weiser Books, 1997.

I Won't Learn from You, by Herbert Kohl, The New Press, 1994.

Jesus and Buddha: The Parallel Sayings, edited by Marcus Borg, Ulysses Press, 1997.

The Kingdom Within: The Inner Meanings of Jesus' Sayings, by John A. Sanford, Paulist Press, 1970.

Living Buddha, Living Christ, by Thich Nhat Hanh, Riverhead, 1995.

Loving-Kindness: The Revolutionary Art of Happiness, by Sharon Salzburg, Shambhala, 1995.

Magical Child: Nature's Plan for Our Children, by Joseph Chilton Pearce, Plume, 1992.

Magical Passes: The Practical Wisdom of the Shamans of Ancient Mexico, by Carlos Castaneda, HarperPerennial, 1998.

Medicine Women, **Curanderas,** *and Women Doctors,* by Bobette Perrone, H. Henrietta Stockel, and Victoria Krueger, University of Oklahoma Press, 1989.

Meditations with Animals, by Gerald Hausman, Bear & Company, 1986.

Metaphysical Bible Dictionary, Unity School of Christianity, 1931.

Mythical Journeys/Legendary Quests, by Moyra Caldecott and illustrated by Cheryl Yambrach Rose, Blandford, England, 1988.

The Myth of Freedom and the Way of Meditation, by Chögyam Trungpa, Shambhala Dragon Editions, Shambhala Publications, 1988.

The Nag Hammadi Library: The Definitive New Translation of the Gnostic Scriptures, by James M. Robinson, general editor, HarperSanFrancisco, 1978.

Native American Myths, by Diana Ferguson, Collins & Brown, 2001.

Native American Stories, Told by Joseph Bruchac, from Keepers of the Earth, by Michael J. Caduto and Joseph Bruchac, Fulcrum Publishing, 1991.

Navaho Indian Myths, by Aileen O'Bryan, 1925 (reprint: *The Dine: Origin Myths of the Navaho Indians,* Smithsonian Institute, Bureau of American Ethnology Bulletin 13, 1956).

Navajo and Tibetan Sacred Wisdom: The Circle of the Spirit, by Peter Gold, Inner Traditions, 1994.

Northern Tales: Traditional Stories of Eskimo and Indian Peoples, selected and edited by Howard Norman, Pantheon Books, 1990.

Opening to Shakti, by Rick Jarow, audiotape, Sounds True, 2000.

The Path to Snowbird Mountain, by Traveller Bird, Farrar, Straus, & Giroux, 1972.

A Path with Heart: A Guide Through the Perils and Promises of Spiritual Life, by Jack Kornfield, Bantam Books, 1993.

The Principles of Psychic Protection, by Judy Hall, Thorsons, 1999.

Psychic Roots: Serendipity and Intuition in Genealogy, by Henry Z. Jones, Genealogical Publishing Company, 1996.

Quantum Healing: Exploring the Frontiers of Mind/Body Medicine, by Deepak Chopra, M.D., Bantam Books, 1990.

Red Earth: Tales of the Micmacs, by Marion Robertson, the Nova Scotia Museum, 1969.

Reinventing Medicine: Beyond Mind-Body to a New Era of Healing, Larry Dossey, M.D., Harper-SanFrancisco, 1999.

Reiki: A Torch in Daylight, by Karyn Mitchell, Mind Rivers Publication, 1994.

Sadhana of the Medicine Buddha, by H. H. Dudjom Rinpoche, Yeshe Melong, 1998.

The Seat of the Soul, by Gary Zukav, Simon and Schuster, 1990.

Secrets of Shamanism: Tapping the Spirit Power Within You, by José Stevens and Lena S. Stevens, Avon, 1988.

Shamanic Voices, by Joan Halifax, Arkana, 1982.

Shamanism, compiled by Shirley Nicholson, the Theosophical Publishing House, 1990.

The Shaman's Body: A New Shamanism for Transforming Health, Relationships, and Community, by Arnold Mindell, Harper-SanFrancisco, 1993.

The Shaman's Doorway: Opening Imagination to Power and Myth, by Stephen Larsen, Inner Traditions, 1999.

Shambhala: The Sacred Path of the Warrior, Chögyam Trungpa, Shambhala Dragon Editions, Shambhala Publications, 1988.

Simple Spells for Success: Ancient Practices for Creating Abundance and Prosperity, by Barrie Dolnick, Harmony Books, 1996.

Somatic Reality: Bodily Experience and Emotional Truth, by Stanley Keleman, Center Press, 1979.

Soul Mates: Honoring the Mysteries of Love and Relationship, by Thomas Moore, HarperPerennial, 1994.

The Soul Would Have No Rainbows If the Eyes Had No Tears, and Other Native American Proverbs, by Guy A. Zona, Simon & Schuster, 1994.

Spinning Inward: Using Guided Imagery with Children for Learning, Creativity & Relaxation, by Maureen Murdock, Shambhala, 1987.

Spirit Practices, by Patricia Mathes Cane, Capacitar Inc., 2000.

Spiritual Intelligence, by Marsha Sinetar, Orbis Books, 2000.

Stalking the Wild Pendulum: On the Mechanics of Consciousness, by Itzhak Bentov, Bantam Books, 1977.

Stories from Around the World, retold by Heather Amery, Usborne, 2000.

Stories of the Spirit, Stories of the Heart: Parables of the Spiritual Path from Around the World, edited by Christina Feldman and Jack Kornfield, HarperCollins, 1991.

The Tao of Physics, by Fritjof Capra, Shambhala, 1975.

The Tao of Psychology, Synchronicity, and the Self, by Jean Shinoda Bolen, M.D., Harper and Row, 1979.

The Teacher-Student Relationship, by Jamgön Kongtrul the Great, translated by Ron Garry, Snow Lion Publications, 1999.

The Teen Spell Book: Magick for Young Witches, by Jamie Wood, Celestial Arts, 2001.

The Thundering Years: Rituals and Sacred Wisdom for Teens, by Julie Tallard Johnson, Bindu Books, 2001.

The Tibetan Book of the Dead: The Great Liberation through Hearing in the Bardo, translated with commentary by Francesca Fremantle & Chögyam Trungpa, Shambhala Publications, 1975.

Tibetan Dream Yoga **(CD)**, by Lama Surya Das, Sounds True, 2000.

The Tibetan Book of Living and Dying, by Sogyal Rinpoche, HarperSanFrancisco. 1992.

Tibetan Buddhist Medicine and Psychiatry: The Diamond Healing, by Terry Clifford, Samuel Weiser, 1984.

The Toltec Path of Recapitulation: Healing Your Past to Free Your Soul, by Victor Sanchez, Bear & Company, 2001.

Training the Mind and Cultivating Loving-Kindness, by Chögyam Trungpa, Shambhala, 2003.

Wake Up to Your Life: Discovering the Buddhist Path of Attention, by Ken McLeod, Harper-SanFrancisco, 2002.

Walking in the Sacred Manner, by Mark St. Pierre and Tilda Long Soldier, Simon & Schuster, 1995.

The Way of The Shaman, by Michael Harner, HarperSanFransisco, 1990.

The Wild Within: Adventures in Nature and Animal Teachings, by Paul Rezendes, Jeremy P. Tarcher/Putnam, 1998.

World Mythology, by Roy Willis, general editor, Owl Books, 1993.

Your Body Speaks Its Mind, by Stanley Keleman, Center Press, 1975.

Your Hands Can Heal, by Ric A. Weinman, E. P. Dutton, 1988.

Zen Mind, Beginner's Mind: Informal Talks on Zen Meditation and Practice, by Shunryu Suzuki, Weatherhill, 1991.

Index